CONTENTS

·MURDEROUS MATHS·

JOIN THE MURDEROUS MATHS GANG
FOR MORE FUN, GAMES AND TIPS AT
www.murderousmaths.co.uk

Also by Kjartan Poskitt:
The Knowledge: The Gobsmacking Galaxy
Dead Famous: Isaac Newton and his Apple

MURDEROUS MATHS

Fractions and Averages
THE MEAN AND VULGAR BITS

KJARTAN POSKITT

Illustrated by
Daniel Postgate

To my lifelong friends Jo, Tom, Bridget and Alice
from your mean and vulgar big brother.

Scholastic Children's Books,
Commonwealth House,
1–19 New Oxford Street,
London WC1A 1NU, UK
a division of Scholastic Ltd
London ~ New York ~ Toronto ~ Sydney ~ Auckland
Mexico City ~ New Delhi ~ Hong Kong

Published by Scholastic Ltd 2000

ISBN 0 439 01270 8

Typeset by TW Typesetting, Midsomer Norton, Somerset
Printed and bound in Denmark by Nørhaven Paperback, Viborg

12 14 16 18 20 19 17 15 13 11

You Have Been Warned

Before you opened this book you should have noticed two things written on the cover. In case you missed them, there is a box at the top which says "Murderous Maths" and the title of the book which is *The Mean and Vulgar Bits*.

It doesn't take a genius to see what these messages are trying to tell you, but in case you are the sort of person who phones up the telly company to complain just because the weatherman hasn't combed his hair, let's make it dead clear:

- Any book with the word "murderous" written on the front is not going to have lots of nice stories about flower arranging, handy hairstyling hints or recipes for fairy cakes in it.

- If a book is called *The Mean and Vulgar Bits*, don't be surprised if you find some mean and vulgar bits inside. Remember that the word "bottom" has two meanings, and in here it is necessary to encounter both of them.

Despite these warnings, there are some people who will still read this book just so they can complain about it...

If you are one of those people, here's a message for you:

As for the rest of us – let's go!

What are mean and vulgar bits?

If you've read a Murderous Maths book called *The Essential Arithmetricks* then you'll already know what vulgar bits are. (You'll also be able to do all sorts of murderous sums *without depending on a calculator*, not to mention lots of other slick stuff.) The vulgar bits were supposed to have had a few chapters to themselves in *The Essential Arithmetricks*, but they were all so badly behaved that they were rounded up and herded off to this maximum security book.

Vulgar bits come from dividing things up. Suppose you have a sum such as $10 \div 5$, the answer comes to 2. In this case the answer is a *whole number* because the answer is exactly 2, there's no nasty little bits left over. However, if your sum was $5 \div 10$, then your answer will be...

As you can see we end up with one number on top of another. This means the answer is not a nice round whole number because $\frac{1}{2}$ is a bit bigger than 0 but it is smaller than 1. Numbers that are not whole numbers are called *fractions*, and thankfully this one is being polite and well behaved.

Oh dear! It's already started being rude, but we'll try and ignore it for now. There are two ways of writing fractions. One way is the decimal fraction which we'll meet properly before too long, but this sort is the...

Be quiet!

That's enough of that.

Sorry about that, but as you may have guessed, this sort of fraction with a number on the top and a number on the bottom is called a *vulgar fraction*.

Mean bits are also pretty disgusting, but in a different sort of way.

Yuk! You'll find out later on why Meanies do nasty things like chop bits of their fingers off, but in the meantime all you need to know is that it's because of fractions. Maybe it was a mistake putting Meanies and fractions in a book together, but it's too late now!

Be prepared

There are some miserable people who will think this book is far too awful/rude/silly/uneducational for you to read, and they may even try to grab the book off you and hide it on top of a dusty cupboard next to a forgotten old hat that was bought to be worn at a wedding but turned out to be the wrong shade of beige. Of course, people like that should mind their own business, so here's how to teach them a lesson.

Before they start lecturing you by saying "That rubbish is a waste of time," or "It will rot your brain," quickly turn to the very back page and show them the "Answers to the terrible test". As you can imagine, those answers are complicated enough to impress even the most obnoxious academic, snooty teacher or grumpy parent. And what's more...

THIS BOOK ABSOLUTELY GUARANTEES THAT AFTER YOU'VE READ THE NEXT 150 PAGES YOU WILL BE ABLE TO WORK OUT ALL THE ANSWERS TO THE TERRIBLE TEST BY YOURSELF IN YOUR HEAD.

There, that should shut them up! All you need to do now is block your auntie's ears and cover up the parrot because here come the...

VERY VULGAR FRACTIONS

Before we find out what to do with these things, we ought to find out why we have to put up with them in the first place. The whole point of fractions is that they tell us exactly how big "bits" of things are and they do this by having one number on top of another. The *numerator* is the number that goes on top...

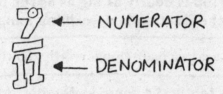

...and the *denominator* is the number that goes on the...

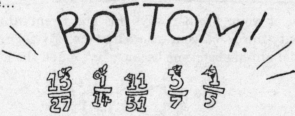

My, aren't they all pleased with themselves for shouting "bottom" right across the page?

A quick guide to the size of fractions

Generally speaking:

> **If the top is a lot smaller than the bottom, then the fraction is describing a very little bit.**

For instance, suppose you have a bar of chocolate you've been saving and your ugly brother comes up and says he's eaten one-sixteenth of it (which looks like $\frac{1}{16}$), then you might decide to let him off with an evil stare. This is because the 1 on the top is a lot smaller than the 16 on the bottom and so the bit he ate wasn't very big. Of course, it's far more likely that he ate something like $\frac{8}{11}$ of the chocolate and in that case it's time to swing on his ears because:

> **If the top is nearly as big as as the bottom, then the fraction is describing a big bit.**

There are two more things worth knowing:

> **If the top is the same as the bottom, then the fraction equals 1.**

So if your brother says he ate twenty-three-twenty-thirds of your chocolate (i.e. $\frac{23}{23}$) then it's spiders-in-his-bed time because he's eaten the lot!

And finally let's look at fractions where the number on top is bigger than the number on the bottom…

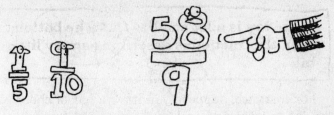

Here's one! This sort is the worst of the lot because:

> **If the number on top is bigger than the number on the bottom, you get an _improper vulgar fraction_!**

The proper way to treat improper fractions

The main problem with improper fractions is that it can be tricky to tell how big they are. Look at this: $\frac{58}{9}$. Is it bigger than 5? Smaller than 20?

How rude! That's why it's usually best to get rid of them, so let's teach this one a lesson. Quick, grab it!

All we need to do is divide the bottom into the top: we get $58 \div 9$, which gives us 6 with a remainder of 4. This means our improper $\frac{58}{9}$ becomes 6 with $\frac{4}{9}$ left over. Let's have a look at it now.

There's still a little vulgar fraction left, but now that we have a big "6" next to it, we have a better idea of what the whole thing is worth – in this case, it's "six and a bit". This mixture of a whole number and a vulgar fraction is called a *mixed fraction*.

Putting improper fractions back together

When you're doing sums with mixed fractions such as $6\frac{4}{9}$, it's often best to swallow your pride, grit your teeth and invite improper fractions back on to the page. What you do is take the whole number (in this case 6) and multiply it by the denominator (the 9 on the bottom) and add the answer to the numerator

14

(the 4 on the top). This sounds ghastly, but here you just multiply 6 by 9, which makes 54, then add that to the 4 to get 58. We just put this 58 over the 9 to get $\frac{58}{9}$ and there we are, all improper again.

Suppose our mixed fraction was $3\frac{1}{2}$: we just multiply the 3 by the 2 to get 6, then add it to the 1 to get 7. In that way $3\frac{1}{2}$ becomes $\frac{7}{2}$.

Right then, now that we've started to show fractions who's in charge, we'll invite a mathematician to explain exactly where fractions come from:

IF YOU HAVE SOMETHING OR A GROUP OF SOMETHINGS THAT YOU WANT TO SPLIT INTO EQUAL PIECES OR LOTS, THEN YOU CAN SHOW IT BY WRITING DOWN THE NUMBER OF SOMETHINGS (OR JUST 'ONE' IF IT'S JUST ONE SOMETHING) AND UNDERNEATH WRITE THE NUMBER OF PIECES OR LOTS YOU WANT TO SPLIT THE SOMETHING OR GROUP OF SOMETHINGS INTO.

Good grief! Let's try and make some sense of this.

Suppose our group of somethings are six dead wildebeests' eyeballs...

And we have three vultures who each want a fair share...

This means we want to split our six eyeballs into three lots. According to our mathematician, we just write down the number of somethings, and underneath we write down the number of lots. Off we go then:

$$\frac{\text{six eyeballs}}{\text{three vultures}}$$

Of course, we could just use numbers and get $\frac{6}{3}$. Yahoo, we've made a fraction! As it turns out, this is an improper fraction so we don't have to put up with it. All we do is divide the bottom into the the top which is $6 \div 3$. This comes out neatly and tells us that each vulture gets two eyeballs.

SLURP

16

As you've realized by now, vulgar fractions are just another way of writing out division sums, and if you like you can imagine the numbers in a division sum creeping on to the dividing sign to make a fraction, like this:

$$6 \div 3 \qquad 6 \rightleftarrows 3 \qquad \frac{6}{3}$$

Do we really have to have fractions?

It's a real shame that all divisions don't just produce nice wholesome round numbers with no nasty bits left over, but they don't. You'd think in these days when all the brainy people have worked out how to blast us with hundreds of channels of widescreen digital telly, they could turn their minds to something as simple as getting rid of fractions, but oh no. They've got better things to think about, haven't they? They think it's more important to make sure every single channel contains nothing but absolute rubbish in stereo so they can bore us into a coma from both sides of the room at once.

No, even as we start our spanking bright new millennium you can't avoid tiny little fractions, even when you start off with some really big numbers. What's more, although big numbers are often harmless, tiny fractions can be murderous...

Scene: The abandoned gas station
Place: Red Ant Prairie, Illinois.
Date: 24 July, 1926
Time: 6.20 a.m.

"There you are boys, ten grand as agreed."

Ma Butcher clicked her fingers, and Long Jake tossed the sack on to the counter next to the spluttering candle. The seven men huddled by the far wall stared, but they all resisted the temptation to run up and grab it. It didn't do to move too suddenly in front of Long Jake. In fact, to be really safe, it didn't do to move at all.

"Thank you kindly, ma'am," muttered Blade Boccelli. "Please don't let us keep you, or Long Jake of course."

"No, not Long Jake," murmured the others. "Don't want to keep Long Jake. Not at all."

Suddenly something glinted in Long Jake's hand. The seven men all dropped to the floor and covered their heads. It was a silver toothpick. Jake leered as he started to pick his silver teeth. Ma Butcher turned to the door.

"Divide it up nice and fair now," she grinned. "Want me to work out what fraction you each get?"

"No thank you, ma'am," muttered Blade, looking out from behind an old oil can. "Ten grand's a whole load of money, so we won't need to be concerned about fractions."

"Whatever you say," said Ma Butcher. "Start the motor, Jake. Nice working with ya, boys."

They were gone. All at once the men were swarming round the table and tugging at the sack.

"Yahoo!" screamed Chainsaw Charlie. "Ten thousand bucks!"

"Funny, ain't it?" said One Finger Jimmy. "Who'd have thought you Gabriannis and us Boccellis would ever work together?"

"Yeah," said Chainsaw. "Even if it was only decorating Ma Butcher's apartment."

There was an embarrassed silence.

"Nobody needs to know about that!" hissed Blade. "We're supposed to be gangsters. If anyone asks, we held up a bank, right?"

"Right!" they all nodded.

"OK, now here's what we agreed," said the Weasel. "There's seven men here and each takes an equal share."

"This sure beats shooting holes in each other," said Porky.

"So to start, I guess we take a thousand each," said the Weasel. "That leaves three thousand on the table."

"But how do we split three thousand between seven?" asked Blade.

"We do it in hundreds," said the Weasel. "And luckily

19

we got just the guy to work it out. Hey Numbers, what do we get?"

"Four hundred each," said the thin man. "And that leaves two hundred dollars on the table."

"At least it's in tens, singles and coins," said Porky Boccelli. "It shouldn't be too hard to divide up."

"So Numbers, out of the two hundred left, how many tens do we get?" asked Chainsaw.

"Two tens," said Numbers.

"Only two?" said Blade. "We just get two tens each out of two hundred dollars?"

"Yeah, you watch it," said Jimmy. "Cos if you Gabriannis are getting any smart ideas..."

Blade, Jimmy and Porky reached for their guns, but too late – they were already looking down the multiple barrels of Half-smile's Dawson-Roach 98.

"Easy you guys!" said the Weasel. "Numbers don't have an idea in his head, he just got numbers. Tell 'em, Numbers..."

"All seven of us take twenty dollars," said Numbers. "That makes one hundred and forty, so

20

out of the two hundred that leaves sixty on the table."

By now there were seven piles of money round the table, each worth $1,420.

"Out of the sixty dollars, we can each take eight," said Numbers. "Which leaves four dollars over."

"What do we do now?" asked Blade.

"Split the dollars into cents, I guess," said Chainsaw.

"Oh brother!" sighed Blade. "You mean even though we started with ten grand, we still have to mess about with a few little cents?"

"Four hundred cents to be accurate," said Numbers. "And we each get 57 of them."

After a lot of laborious shuffling and counting, each man checked his pile.

"I got $1,428 and 57 cents exactly," said Half-smile.

"Me too," said Jimmy. "Same for all of us, but what do we do now?"

Every man was staring towards the middle of the table where one final little coin glinted in the candlelight.

"Maybe I get my saw and chop it into seven pieces," sniggered Chainsaw, not realizing that he'd made the only workable suggestion.

"Don't be a mug," said Blade reaching for the coin. "I'm not messing with little itty-bitty fractions of a cent. The only answer is that I'll take it."

"Oh no you don't!" snapped the Weasel whisking a Pedley Surefire from his belt, but Blade was already through the door.

"After him!" shouted Half-smile to his brothers.

"After them!" shouted Jimmy to Porky.

"After you!" shouted Porky.

Soon they had all burst out into the night, and they would never know whose departing foot it was that had kicked the table and upset the candle. It was a simple chain of events: upset candle, burning banknotes, oil-soaked timber floor, forgotten fuel bunker...

The seven figures span round to see a giant orange fireball light up the sky.

"The gas station!" came a unified cry. "And our *money*!"

On a distant hillside, Long Jake started up the car engine.

"Just like I thought!" chuckled Ma Butcher. "I knew it was worth staying back to watch. Just goes to show, you can't ignore fractions."

Names of fractions

This is easy. Look at the number underneath, and that's how you get the name. $\frac{1}{5}$ is one-fifth, $\frac{1}{12}$ is one-twelfth, $\frac{1}{284}$ is one-two-hundred-and-eighty-fourth, and so on. There are just three exceptions:

$\frac{1}{2}$ is called a *half*. (Once again this book has just revealed a secret that you would never have guessed in your WILDEST dreams.)

$\frac{1}{4}$ is called a *quarter*. This comes from the old Latin word "quartus" which means "fourth". In the old days people used to be hung, drawn and quartered, which meant that they were hung from a gallows, then drawn (this doesn't mean that somebody drew a picture of them, it means they had their insides chopped out) and then sawn into bits. Mind you, there were usually more than four bits by the time the executioner had finished all his encores and curtain calls.

$\frac{1}{100}$ is often called one *per cent*. This comes from Latin too, as anything with "cent" in it means 100. American money has 100 cents in a dollar. Percentages get used a lot and they even have a special sign which is %.

Fractions can be used to describe bits of anything – whether you're sharing out a box of chocolates, chopping a piano into 29 bits or even invading a neighbouring galaxy that wasn't doing you any harm and dividing the stars and planets up between the cosmic commandants of your glorious space fleet.

Funnily enough, even though fractions can apply to almost anything, for some reason people *always* explain fractions by imagining cakes being cut up into absolutely equal pieces like this:

And we're supposed to believe that's what happens in real life. Of course, what *really* happens next is this:

Oh well, cakes are still the easiest way to see about fractions so we'll make some cakes and see how we get on.

RECIPE FOR FAIRY CAKES

Good grief! This is supposed to be a book about Murderous Maths, and yet a recipe for fairy cakes nearly managed to sneak in. We don't need to be told how to do soppy stuff like that, instead we'll just mix up whatever we can find in the cupboard. We'll use margarine, eggs, milk, cornflakes, barbecue sauce, sugar, baked beans, lard, coffee, jam...

We've got enough mix for two cakes, so we'll divide it into two tins and plonk them in the oven and turn it right up full to save time. Hmm! It smells good already, but don't forget this is a maths experiment. While the cakes are cooking we need to buy a load of cherries from that nice little old lady who lives in the cave with her raven and her talking cat.

Hello! What's this? A piece of paper has fluttered out of the cherry bag. It says:

> *One for a sneeze, two for a twitch,*
> *Three for a spot and four for an itch,*
> *Five for a head covered in feathers,*
> *Six for a day with the worst of all weathers,*
> *Seven for laughter, eight for sorrow,*
> *Nine for sleep until tomorrow,*
> *Ten for tiny, eleven for big,*
> *Twelve or more: turn into a pig.*

All very quaint, but what's that got to do with Murderous Maths, eh? Absolutely nothing, so let's get on because our cakes have baked already. Doesn't time fly when you're reading a book?

Right it's time to put the cherries round the top of the cakes. It looks like we can fit 24 round the first one.

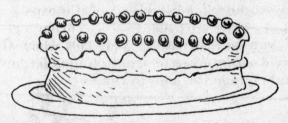

Let's mark this cake into three equal pieces and cut one of the pieces out. By now you've realized that this piece is one-third of the whole cake, and so we should be able to work out how many cherries are on it. What makes it fun is that there are two ways of doing this.

- As we divided our cake by 3, the number of cherries we get on one piece is $24 \div 3$.
- As we have one-third *of* a cake, we can just multiply $24 \times \frac{1}{3}$. To explain this we'll pinch one of the *Essential Arithmetricks* which says...

With fractions, "of" means "multiplied by".

Of course, both answers come to eight cherries which we can check if we look at our cake.

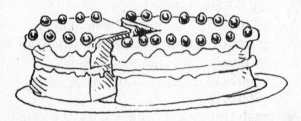

What is exciting is that because these two sums come up with the same answer, they must be equal to each other: $24 \div 3 = 24 \times \frac{1}{3}$.

In other words dividing by 3 is the same as multiplying by $\frac{1}{3}$. This demonstrates one of the best ways to deal with nasty little vulgar fractions:

> **If you are dividing, you can turn the dividing number or fraction upside down and change the sign to times!**

Sadly, that doesn't help much. You have to think of it more like this: first you imagine the 3 has a 1 underneath, so it turns into the little fraction $\frac{3}{1}$. There's nothing wrong with putting a 1 under any number, and you'll see that if you work this fraction out you get: $3 \div 1$ which comes back to 3 again. So when we have the sum $24 \div 3$, all you do is think of it as $24 \div \frac{3}{1}$. Then you can turn the $\frac{3}{1}$ upside down. That way $\div \frac{3}{1}$ becomes $\times \frac{1}{3}$.

Sometimes it's helpful if you can get rid of dividing signs from sums, and this little trick works with any number you like. For instance:

$538 = 2561418 \div 4761$ is the same as

$538 = 2561418 \times \frac{1}{4761}$

Although this might not seem terribly useful just now, when fractions get fancier you'll find turning things upside down can make life much easier.

Right then, let's get back to the cake...

Gosh, that was a big sneeze. Anyway, who wants this bit of cake with eight cherries on?

Try to stop sneezing and twitching, you two. What's got into you, anyway? We'll go on...

Because we've given away one-third of our cake, we still have two-thirds left over. We can write two-thirds like this: $\frac{2}{3}$. So how many cherries are left on two-thirds of the cake?

We had 24 cherries to start with, so we just multiply that by $\frac{2}{3}$. The sum looks like this: $24 \times \frac{2}{3}$. Here it helps to remember that 24 can be written as $\frac{24}{1}$, so we can write the sum out as $\frac{24}{1} \times \frac{2}{3}$. Here's another handy tip to know:

> **To multiply fractions, just multiply the tops together and put them on top. Then multiply the bottoms together and put them on the bottom!**

Here's how it goes...

$$\frac{24 \times 2}{1 \times 3} = \frac{48}{3}$$

Of course $\frac{48}{3}$ is the same as $48 \div 3$ so we can tidy it up by working it out and getting the answer – there are 16 cherries left. Let's check...

Well that's what we expected because we started with 24 cherries, there were 8 cherries in the piece we gave away, so $24 - 8$ leaves 16. Hooray! Our fractions seem to be working.

BOO HOOO
BOO HOOO!

What's the matter with him? First we have sneezing, then twitching, and now uncontrollable sobbing!

Right, let's look at the other cake which also has 24 cherries on it.

ER, NO. NOT QUITE 24.

TO BE HONEST, WHEN WE WERE PUTTING THE CHERRIES ON I ATE ONE AND SHE ATE TWO ATTISSHOOO!

Oh. So that means we only have 21 cherries on our second cake. Never mind. This time we'll do some slightly fancier cutting. Let's mark our cake out into seven equal pieces, then cut two of them out!

How many cherries are on the *two* pieces? Simple – each piece of cake is one-seventh of the cake, and we have two of them. So the sum is two-sevenths times

21 which we can write like this: $\frac{21}{1} \times \frac{2}{7}$. That's not too bad to work out because we get $\frac{42}{7}$, and of course $42 \div 7 = 6$. Later on we'll see how to make these sums even simpler by "cancelling out", but for now we have six cherries on two bits of cake, so who wants them?

Our second cake has 15 cherries left, so let's smooth the icing over…

…then mark the rest of the cake into three pieces and take one away.

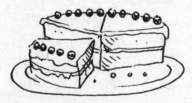

Not too hard to work out how many cherries are on this piece – it's $15 \times \frac{1}{3}$, which comes to 5 cherries. Who's going to eat that?

We have ten cherries left on the cake, so just for fun we'll divide it into five bits, and give two of them to somebody. By now you'll easily see they get $10 \times \frac{2}{5}$ cherries which comes to 4.

Well that's about it for cakes now. Let's just see for interest what we've got left. There are 6 cherries on the second cake, and ... gosh where's the first cake gone? Some greedy person has eaten it!

33

Never mind cake, let's get on to jelly

Suppose you are making jellies and have four litres of jelly mixture. First let's see how much mixture each jelly mould needs:

So now we can work out how many jellies we can make. All we need to ask ourselves is, "How many lots of 2 litres can we get out of four litres?" Which is the same as asking what is $4 \div 2$, so the answer is that we can make two jellies.

That $\frac{2}{3}$ looks nasty – let's have a close-up...

Urghh! but don't worry because the only difference it makes to our sum is that instead of $4 \div 2$, we get $4 \div \frac{2}{3}$. Don't forget how we can easily divide by vulgar fractions. We just flip them upside

34

down and change the sign to times! In this case we find the number of jellies we can make $= 4 \times \frac{3}{2}$. That comes to $\frac{12}{2}$ which gives an answer of 6 jellies!

Silly fractions

Of course, if you want to be really fancy when you work out the jelly sum, you could start with $4 \div \frac{2}{3}$ and move the numbers on to the sign (as we saw on page 17) to make it like this:

$$\frac{4}{\frac{2}{3}}$$

The important thing here is to make sure the line under the 4 is bigger than the line between the 2 and the 3. Otherwise people might think you've written:

$$\frac{\frac{4}{2}}{3}$$

Which means $\frac{4}{2} \div 3$ and is completely different. (One of them comes to 6 and the other comes to $\frac{2}{3}$. Check them if you like!)

This can get even sillier. Suppose you had wanted to write $\frac{23}{25} \div \frac{11}{16}$ as a really big fraction, you could make it into this:

OOOPS! HOLD STILL!

I CAN'T HELP IT. YOUR BOTTOM'S RIGHT BY MY NOSE!

... which looks even wobblier than the jellies!

Space Camouflage

By now you'll have realized that most of the sums you have to do aren't too hard, especially if they are written out on a bit of paper to start with. All the numbers and operators are there, you just have to mush them all up and get an answer.

Unfortunately, in everyday life sums don't usually turn up on bits of paper. It's far more common to have to think about a situation and work out what sum you need to do. Will it be adding, subtracting, multiplying, or dividing? What numbers are needed? Where do the numbers go? Of course while you're pondering such great thoughts, who knows what might be happening in the distant skies above you…

Any day now, it's quite likely that everybody will be asked to paint massive stars all over their house to protect us from an invasion craft from the planet

Zog. The plan is that if the whole of Earth is painted in stars, it will blend in with the rest of the sky and they'll miss us. Clever, eh?

Right then, we've got two pots of paint, so let's see how many stars we can get from them.

Oh dear. Two pots were only enough to paint 4 of the 5 points of a star, so in other words they only did $\frac{4}{5}$ of it. But how many pots would we need for a whole star?

Before we go on, we can get a hint from using one of the smartest tools in maths: *your own common sense!* Two pots were nearly enough to do the job, but not quite. The answer we are looking for is a bit more than two! Have a guess – what do you think it might be?

Here's how to work it out properly. We know that two pots covered $\frac{4}{5}$ of one star. Remember that with fractions "of" means multiplied by, so we can make this into a sort of equation: 2 pots = 1 star $\times \frac{4}{5}$.

So far so good, but what we want to do is rearrange the equation so that we just have "1 star" on one side and everything else on the other. If you've read *The Essential Arithmetricks* you'll know we can use the trick of swapping the $\times \frac{4}{5}$ over and changing the sign to give us $\div \frac{4}{5}$, but for fun let's check how it works. The main thing to know is that *you must treat both sides of an equation the same*.

In this case we'll divide both sides by $\frac{4}{5}$ which gives us: 2 pots $\div \frac{4}{5} = 1$ star $\times \frac{4}{5} \div \frac{4}{5}$.

Anything divided by itself comes to 1, so the $\frac{4}{5} \div \frac{4}{5}$ comes to 1 which leaves us with: 2 pots $\div \frac{4}{5} = 1$ star.

Hey, we're dividing by fractions which is easy! We just turn them upside down and multiply to get: 2 pots $\times \frac{5}{4} = 1$ star.

We've found out that the number of pots we need for one star is $2 \times \frac{5}{4}$ which comes to $\frac{10}{4}$ and if you work out $10 \div 4$, you find that you need $2\frac{1}{2}$ pots of paint for one star. Is that what you guessed?

IF I CAN FIT 7 STARS ON OUR HOUSE, HOW MANY POTS OF PAINT WILL I NEED ALTOGETHER?

Simple! Each star needs $2\frac{1}{2}$ pots, so for 7 stars you need $7 \times 2\frac{1}{2}$ pots. To work this out, you can choose how you'd like to do it:

- You can do the bits separately because sums like this are just the same as other multiplications. First of all, multiply up the halves to get $7 \times \frac{1}{2} = \frac{7}{2}$, which is the same as $3\frac{1}{2}$ pots. Next, multiply up the whole pots and get $7 \times 2 = 14$ pots. Finally, add the two answers together and get $14 + 3\frac{1}{2} = 17\frac{1}{2}$ pots.

- You convert the $2\frac{1}{2}$ pots into an improper fraction, which comes to $\frac{5}{2}$. The sum is then $7 \times \frac{5}{2} = \frac{35}{2}$. We can then convert $\frac{35}{2}$ back. We find that 2 goes into

35 seventeen times with a remainder of 1, so we get $17\frac{1}{2}$.

So $17\frac{1}{2}$ pots of paint later…

BLINKIN' AWKWARD NUMBERS

Even if you are as tough as an old boot, you have to admit that it would be nice to have a rest from fractions now, wouldn't it?

YEAH.

Here's something to make you pleased then...

GUARANTEE: This chapter only contains *whole* numbers.

What's even better is that we're going to see how some numbers can help us clean up even the meanest and vulgarest bits of maths, and it all starts with one of the most fundamental, crucial, trouser-drenchingly exciting facts of maths which is: **Some numbers are easier to divide into than others.**

It's only nine words long but in the maths world this sentence is BIG BIG BIG so let's see what the fuss is about.

12 is a really nice number because you can divide it by 1,2,3,4,6 and 12 without getting any remainder or a nasty fraction. Numbers that divide exactly into another number are called *factors*, and so the factors of 12 are 1,2,3,4,6 and 12. This is why you can often buy things in twelves, because there's lots of neat ways of packing them in boxes.

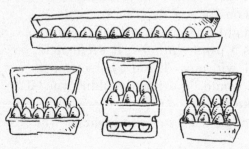

Other numbers are blinkin' awkward to divide into. Take the number 13 for example – it's only one more than 12, but when you try to split it up, it's a real pig. There are only two division sums you can do with 13 that don't have a remainder or a fraction:

$13 \div 1 = 13$

$13 \div 13 = 1$

This means there's only one way of neatly packing 13 things into a box:

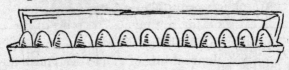

If you try boxes that are shorter and wider, you'll always end up with empty spaces, or things left over.

There are tons and tons of awkward numbers that can only be divided exactly by themselves and one, and these are called *prime numbers*. The smallest prime number is 2, because if you think about it, 2 will only divide exactly by 1 or 2. The next prime numbers are 3,5,7,11,13,17,19,23,29,31... and the list goes on for ever.

You might have noticed that the number 1 is not listed as a prime number. It seems odd, because of course 1 will only divide by itself or one, so you'd think it would be prime, wouldn't you? This might seem like a silly point, but there are people in the world called pure mathematicians who absolutely *love* prime numbers, and they have deep intellectual debates about the number 1…

(In this chapter, it's handy for us to think that 1 is *not* a prime number, so we'll be sensible and just think about the other prime numbers.)

Although prime numbers are very irritating when you have to divide them up, they can be extremely useful for sorting out other divisions and even vulgar fractions. This is because of one rather marvellous thing about them:

> **Any number that is not prime can be made by multiplying two or more prime numbers together.**

An easy example is the number 15. This can be made by multiplying together 3 and 5, which are both prime numbers. Because they are prime numbers and they are factors, can you guess what they are called? Yes, they are *prime factors*.

A more interesting number is 24, which can be made by multiplying together 6 and 4. Neither 6 nor 4 are prime numbers, but you can split 6 into 3×2 and you can split 4 into 2×2. This means we can get 24 from $3 \times 2 \times 2 \times 2$, so that means we've split 24 into its prime factors.

Of course, 24 can also be made by multiplying together 3 and 8. 3 is a prime number but 8 isn't because you can make it with 2×4. We're getting closer, because 2 is a prime number, but 4 isn't! However, you can make 4 from 2×2. This means that you can get 8 from $2 \times 2 \times 2$, so you can get 24 from $3 \times 2 \times 2 \times 2$. Gosh! We've split 24 into exactly the same prime factors as when we started with 6×4!

Here's where the prime numbers get useful, because every number has its own set of prime factors. It's a bit like having your own personal identity code – you only have one code which says who you are, and nobody else has the same one as you.

If you check a nice number like 36, you'll find it can be made from 6×6, or it can come from 9×4 (or it can even come from 3×12). It doesn't matter which way you start dividing it up, when you keep going and finally break it down into its prime factors, you'll get $36 = 2 \times 2 \times 3 \times 3$.

Here are some numbers with their prime factors:

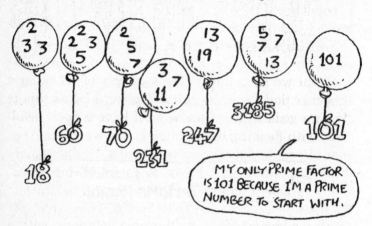

MY ONLY PRIME FACTOR IS 101 BECAUSE I'M A PRIME NUMBER TO START WITH.

Security alert

DANG-A-LANG-A-LANG!

Wow, what a racket! The alarm bell has just gone off at TransWorld International Trading Systems – apparently the toilet window has been broken and the security guards are looking into it. They have found a set of footprints, so an intruder is at large! This calls for a special investigator who knows a few arithmetricks.

Luckily, everybody at TWITS wears an ID badge with a number on it. None of the genuine numbers have more than three prime factors, so can you unmask the intruder?

What we need now is the best way of breaking a number down into its prime factors, and as this is such a good thing to know we'll have a posh headline with flashing lights:

HOW TO BREAK A NUMBER DOWN INTO ITS PRIME FACTORS

To see how we do it, we'll grab a volunteer with a low ID number.

I'VE BEEN WORKING FOR TWITS SINCE THE LAST ICE AGE

You'll do!

YOWKS!

CLOSE UP OF JANITOR'S ID

68

His number is 68, and what we do is try and divide this by the prime numbers in turn, starting with the lowest one, which is 2. If you're feeling feeble you can use a calculator – but remember you only want answers that are nice round numbers. *If a prime does not divide into your number exactly, then that prime is not a factor.* For those of us who think calculators are for wimps, here's a few handy tips:

- *Any even number will divide by 2.* (But odd numbers won't!)
- *A number will only divide by 3 if the digital root will divide by 3.*

  Digital roots are good fun. All you do is add all the digits of your number together, so if your number is 27483, add up $2+7+4+8+3$ and get 24. You then go on to add up the 2 and the 4 to get 6. When you've only got one digit left, that's the digital root! In this case our digital root is 6 which will divide by three, and that means 27483 will divide by three too!

- *A number will only divide by 5 if it ends in a 0 or a 5.*

Let's get started on 68, and we'll keep a list of the prime factors as we go along:

CLEVER THOUGHTS AND SUMS	PRIME FACTOR
68 is even so we can divide it by 2 to start with: $68 \div 2 = 34$	2
Now that we've divided by 2, we see that we've got 34 left, so we keep	

trying to split that into more factors. Because 34 is also even we get another prime factor of 2: $34 \div 2 = 17$	**2**
17 won't divide by 2, but how about 3? Let's find the digital root: $1 + 7 = 8$. No good! 8 won't divide by 3, so 17 will not divide by 3 either. This means that 3 is not a prime factor.	
Will 17 divide by 5? Do fish wear swimming trunks? Of course not because it doesn't end in 5 or 0. So 5 isn't a prime factor.	
Will 17 divide by 7? Only one way to find out, try and do it ... but $17 \div 7$ comes to 2 and a bit left over, so 7 isn't a prime factor either.	
You could go on to try dividing by the next prime numbers which are 11 then 13 ... but you can save time by realizing that the prime number after that is 17. This means that 17 must be the last prime factor!	**17**

We've proved the janitor is not the culprit because his number only has three prime factors: 2, 2 and 17. You can always do a quick check by multiplying $2 \times 2 \times 17$ and making sure you get 68!

Right then, it's your turn to attack the ID numbers and see which one has more than 3 prime factors!

THE RECORDS SHOW THAT ONE OF THE ID NUMBERS ONLY HAS TWO PRIME FACTORS BUT THEY ARE BOTH PRETTY BIG. FINDING THEM COULD BE MURDEROUS.

Are prime factors any use at all to anyone ever?

Oh yes indeedy-doo-dah.

We'll come back to how prime factors can give hope to your soul and joy to your heart later on, but now for a quick trick...

A prime prediction!

Ask a friend to choose any prime number except 2 or 3, but they mustn't let you know what it is. Here's what they do:

- Multiply the prime number by itself
- Add 14
- Divide by 12
- Without knowing which number they started with, you can tell them that they get a remainder of 3! Or if they did the sum on a calculator, you can tell them that the answer ends in "·25"

This works with a little prime number such as 7:

$7 \times 7 = 49$ then $49 + 14 = 63$.

$63 \div 12$ goes 5 times with a remainder of 3.

It also works with big prime numbers such as 1879.

$1879 \times 1879 = 3530641$

$3530641 + 14 = 3530655$

$3530655 \div 12 = 294221 \cdot 25$

THE BUG BUSTER

Spring cleaning your calculator?

Think you've got it perfectly clean, don't you?

Oops, there's still a few bugs under that mouldy silicon chip. And you couldn't get rid of them, could you?

Of course not. Let's see why...

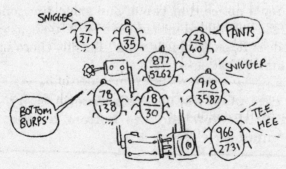

Aha! You've got a vulgar epidemic, and if you're not careful it'll clog the works up and make even the simplest sums into nightmares. You must get rid of these as soon as you can, or you'll suffer from the deadly "Un-understandable Equation" syndrome. Luckily help is at hand with three new products:

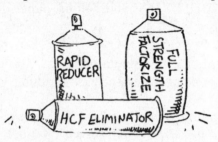

Let's try a spray of "Rapid Reducer" first, and see what we get.

Aha! You'll notice that two of our tough fractions have already crumbled into much nicer little beasts. So how does Rapid Reducer work? Luckily there's a rule in maths that says:

> **You can play about with fractions by dividing the top and the bottom by the same number.**

50

(Or if you prefer it, you can multiply the top and the bottom by the same number.)

Let's see what happened to the $\frac{7}{21}$. All the Rapid Reducer did was to take our nasty looking fraction and divide both the top and the bottom by the smaller of the two numbers which in this case was 7. If you wanted to do it yourself on paper, it might look like this:

$$\frac{\cancel{7}^{\,1}}{\cancel{21}_{\,3}}$$

On the top line we get $7 \div 7 = 1$ and on the bottom we get $21 \div 7 = 3$ so we finish up with a much nicer $\frac{1}{3}$. Cool maths dudes have a few hip and groovy words to describe this. They would say that $\frac{7}{21}$ has been "*reduced*" to $\frac{1}{3}$ and it happened because we *cancelled through* by 7.

You will notice that $\frac{877}{5262}$ also turned into $\frac{1}{6}$, because by an amazing stroke of luck it turns out that $5262 \div 877 = 6$.

PIG SNOT!

You're wondering about the other nasty fractions, aren't you? For more stubborn fractions you might like to try the "HCF Eliminator". Let's spray one with it and see what we get:

HCF Eliminator is a cleverer version of Rapid Reducer. It works by finding the highest number that will divide into both the top and bottom of a fraction. In fact "HCF" stands for Highest Common Factor, and in this case the HCF of $\frac{28}{40}$ is the number 4. Once you know what the HCF is, you just cancel through by 4 and get:

$$\frac{\cancel{28}^{7}}{\cancel{40}^{10}}$$

(You'll notice that the HCF doesn't have to be a prime factor, it just has to be the biggest factor.)

So how do you know what the HCF of two numbers is? The secret is that you need to know the times tables. Let's see if we can deal with the $\frac{18}{30}$ without using the HCF spray.

52

Yes, you can divide top and bottom by 3, but actually you can do better than that because in this case the HCF is *not* 3. When you think about it a bit more you'll realize...

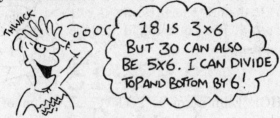

THWACK

18 IS 3×6 BUT 30 CAN ALSO BE 5×6. I CAN DIVIDE TOP AND BOTTOM BY 6!

Bingo! Let's try it...

Nice one! But what happens when we have to deal with fractions like $\frac{78}{138}$? You can't be expected to know about numbers like that in the times tables! It's time to pull on the rubber gloves and face mask, because we're going to have to resort to "Full Strength Factorize". Let's give the $\frac{78}{138}$ a blast and see what happens.

YA!

$\frac{78}{138}$

WOW

$\frac{2 \times 3 \times 13}{2 \times 3 \times 23}$

Yes, Full Strength Factorize breaks the numbers in your fraction down into their prime factors! (If you want to check, you'll find that $2 \times 3 \times 13$ becomes 78 and $2 \times 3 \times 23$ becomes 138 again.) Now quickly, before the little devil reforms himself, we blast him with our Rapid Reducer and watch for some magic results!

$$\frac{\cancel{2} \times \cancel{3} \times 13}{\cancel{2} \times \cancel{3} \times 23}$$

Got him! Rapid Reducer has got rid of his common factors! First it found there was a two on both the top and the bottom lines, so it cancelled them out. (This is the same as dividing both the top and the bottom by 2.) Then it found a three on both top and bottom, so they got cancelled out too! This leaves us with a harmless little fraction that's much easier to deal with.

$$\frac{13}{23}$$

OK let's try Full Strength Factorize on the others...

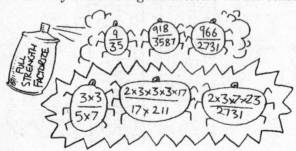

54

All the numbers have been turned into their prime factors. "Aha!" you're thinking, "But what about 2731". Well unfortunately there are some numbers that even Full Strength Factorize can't touch because they are already prime. 2731 is a prime number, and for that matter so is 211 which wouldn't break down any further. Right then, we'll have a quick blast of Rapid Reducer to get rid of the numbers that cancel and we get:

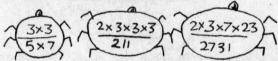

Sadly that's as far down as these fractions will go. We'll just wait until they reform themselves by multiplying their surviving factors back up, then we can compare them with how they started:

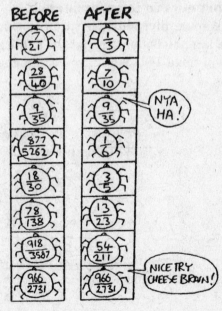

Out of the eight fractions we started with, there are only two that couldn't be reduced. Both the top and bottom of $\frac{9}{35}$ factorized nicely, but there weren't any common factors. As for the other survivor, although 966 factorized beautifully, sadly the prime 2731 beat us.

Still, not a bad result. So, will you be using Rapid Reducer, HCF Eliminator and Full Strength Factorize now?

Short cuts in long divisions!
Of course, divisions are just the same as fractions, and long divisions are just the same as big fractions. If you have $1617 \div 462$, you could charge into it like this:

...and get an answer of $3\frac{231}{462}$ which you'll eventually realize will reduce to $3\frac{1}{2}$.

Of course, the much cooler thing to do is to factorize the two numbers to start with. You'll find that...

$$\frac{1617}{462} = \frac{3 \times 7 \times 7 \times 11}{2 \times 3 \times 7 \times 11}$$

Great! You can cancel out a "$\times 3$", a "$\times 7$" and a "$\times 11$" from both top and bottom. This leaves you with just $\frac{7}{2}$, giving you the answer $3\frac{1}{2}$. Isn't that just super?

When you get really slick, you needn't bother factorizing the whole thing to start with, you can just reduce it in easy stages. All you do is work through the prime numbers in turn (starting with 2) and see if you can divide both top and bottom by them. In this case you look at $\frac{1617}{462}$ but because 1617 is odd, obviously it won't divide by 2.

WAH! WAS DIVIDING BY **2** SO MUCH TO ASK?!

$$\frac{1617}{462}$$

Hey, don't let them see you're upset! Just move on and see if you can divide through by 3 next. Quickly check the digital root of 1617 and you get $1+6+1+7=15$ and then $1+5=6$. Great! As 6 divides by 3, then so does 1617. If you check 462, you'll find it divides by 3 as well! This means that we can divide through by 3 and get:

$$\frac{\cancel{1617}}{\cancel{462}} \quad \frac{539}{154}$$

GOTCHA!

You should try 3 hoping that it might go again ... but in this case it won't and neither will 5. However, when you try 7...

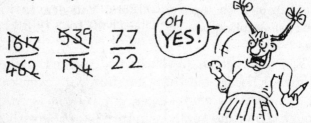

$$\frac{\cancel{1617}}{\cancel{462}} \quad \frac{\cancel{539}}{\cancel{154}} \quad \frac{77}{22}$$

OH YES!

When you try 7 again you'll find it goes into the top, but not the bottom so that's no good. The next prime number is 11, so try that...

$$\frac{\cancel{1617}}{\cancel{462}} \quad \frac{\cancel{539}}{\cancel{154}} \quad \frac{\cancel{77}}{\cancel{22}} \quad \frac{7}{2}$$

♪ YOU'RE FEEBLE AND YOU KNOW IT ♪

It's a great feeling, isn't it? All we're left with is $\frac{7}{2}$, which is the answer we got before.

Although you need to do a lot of little divisions when you are reducing big fractions, once you've managed to divide through by the easy numbers like two and three then the whole thing starts to crumble apart. Reducing is well worth the effort because a number like $3\frac{1}{2}$ is much nicer to work with than $\frac{1617}{462}$!

NEWSFLASH
VULGAR BITS ARE REVOLTING!

WE INTERRUPT THIS BOOK TO BRING YOU SOME ALARMING NEWS ABOUT VULGAR FRACTIONS.

IT SEEMS THEY ARE EXTREMELY UPSET AT HOW SIMPLE MURDEROUS MATHS READERS ARE FINDING THEM.

SO THEY HAVE FORMED THEMSELVES INTO A SUM THAT IS SO DIABOLICALLY DIFFICULT THAT JUST ONE LOOK AT IT CAN MAKE YOUR HEAD MELT.

READERS ARE ADVISED TO PROCEED WITH THE UTMOST CAUTION!

Oh no! Can you hear some suspicious sniggering coming from over the page? What can it be? Maybe it's just too murderous to contemplate. Whatever you do, don't turn the page...

Argh! You turned the page! And look...

It's horrible, it's ugly, and worst of all it's completely pointless! Ridiculous sums like this never turn up in real life, so we won't let this sad little bunch waste our time.

Tum tee tum. We're ignoring you. Lah-di-dah...

Cowards? NOBODY calls us cowards! OK, if it's a fight they want, then they can have one. First we'll limber up by getting rid of any mixed fractions such as $1\frac{2}{15}$. We just convert them into improper fractions and get this:

$$\frac{17}{15} \times \frac{6}{7} \times \frac{49}{143} \div \frac{14}{9} \times \frac{22}{3} \div \frac{17}{5}$$

Now we'll have a little knockabout and get rid of any dividing signs by just turning the dividing fraction upside down. We get this:

$$\frac{17}{15} \times \frac{6}{7} \times \frac{49}{143} \times \frac{9}{14} \times \frac{22}{3} \times \frac{5}{17}$$

We're almost ready to land the big punches, but first we'll soften it up by factorizing all the numbers.

$$\frac{17}{3 \times 5} \times \frac{2 \times 3}{7} \times \frac{7 \times 7}{11 \times 13} \times \frac{3 \times 3}{2 \times 7} \times \frac{2 \times 11}{3} \times \frac{5}{17}$$

Right, it's time to sharpen that pencil and come out of the corner swinging! We're going to do some serious cancelling out now. If *any* number on the top has a matching partner *anywhere* on the bottom, we can knock them both out! We'll start at the beginning of the top line and keep bashing our way along. Wa-hey, off we go…

 The first number on the top is a 17. Is there one on the bottom? Yes, so we can knock them right off the planet by crossing them both out.

 The next number along the top is a 2, and yes there's a 2 on the bottom as well. Say bye-bye to them both!

 Next there's a 3, so we can take it out along with one of the 3's on the bottom.

 Next we find a 7 on top and a 7 on the bottom, so they're both history.

 Hey, there's another 7 on the top and another on the bottom, so we bury them both.

61

We reach another 3, and there's still one more 3 on the bottom. So long, kiddos!

Next we come to yet another 3, but there aren't any more 3's on the bottom to cancel it with. Unfortunately, this 3 has to stay, and so does the 2 after it because there are no 2's left on the bottom either.

 With a blistering finish we can get rid of the 11's from top and bottom, and also the 5's.

We've reached the end of the line, so let's step back and admire our handiwork.

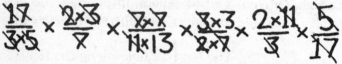

We can see that the only survivors to our onslaught are a rather pitiful 3×2 on the top and a lonely 13 on the bottom. By the time the remains of this sum have been patched up it just comes to $\frac{6}{13}$. We are victorious!

If you get really familiar with numbers, you can do sums like this without bothering to do the factorizing. Suppose you start with this:

$$1\frac{2}{7} \times 2\frac{2}{3} \div 3\frac{3}{7}$$

When you make it into improper fractions and flip the dividing fraction over you get...

$$\frac{9}{7} \times \frac{8}{3} \times \frac{7}{24}$$

Can you work out what this comes to in your head?

Obviously the 7's cancel out.

$$\frac{9}{\cancel{7}_1} \times \frac{8}{3} \times \frac{\cancel{7}^1}{24}$$

If you know the times tables, you'll realize that the 8 on the top divides into the 24 three times, so you can imagine the sum has turned into this...

$$\frac{9}{1} \times \frac{\cancel{8}^1}{3} \times \frac{1}{\cancel{24}} {}_3$$

Then you see that there are two threes on the bottom. Of course when they multiply together you get $3 \times 3 = 9$, and so they cancel with the 9 on the top.

$$\frac{\cancel{9}_1}{1} \times \frac{1}{\cancel{3}_1} \times \frac{1}{\cancel{3}} {}_1$$

The answer comes to exactly 1. Isn't that satisfying?

AHH! THAT FELT GOOD.

BROTHERLY LOVE AND THE LCD

Scene: Luigi's diner
Place: Upper Main St, Chicago, Illinois
Date: 30 December, 1926
Time: 9.45 p.m.

"You got all that, Luigi?" came a voice from the shadowy booth in the corner.

"Er ... I think so, Mr Boccelli!" replied Luigi nervously, as he scribbled on the pad by his till.

There was nobody else in the joint. Just Luigi, Benni the waiter and the three stony-faced men who always sat away from the light, masked in a haze of cigar smoke. The leader of the group spoke again.

"So read it back," said Blade.

"You want a New Year party," said Luigi. "And there's going to be twelve members of the Boccelli family here."

"Yeah, they're all coming," said One Finger Jimmy. "It's the season of goodwill and brotherly love. Besides, they know it ain't healthy to refuse a family invitation."

"But you say you invited the Gabrianni brothers too?" asked Luigi.

"We had to," said Blade. "They could be upset if they were left out."

"But you guys are sworn enemies!" grunted Benni who was heaving a mountainous tray-load of food on to the table.

"We are competing businessmen," said Blade.

"That's right!" said Porky Boccelli as he grabbed a couple of chickens and a rack of cow ribs and tried to shove them into a small bread roll. "It's just that in our business competition is fierce."

"Do you want some more bread rolls?" asked Benni.

"No, the doc told me to cut back," explained Porky. "I only get one teeny sandwich for lunch."

"Blade, please!" begged Luigi. "Whenever the Boccellis and the Gabriannis meet in here, the damage puts me out of business for months."

"Relax, Luigi!" said Blade. "Like Jimmy says, it's the season of goodwill, and besides we did pull a decorating job together!"

"A decorating job?" gasped Luigi.

"Bank job!" snapped Blade. "Bank bank bank. You heard wrong. Not decorating, but BANK!"

"The point is…" interrupted Jimmy, "if we invite them they'll come through the door in their tuxedos. If we don't, they'll come through the wall in their bulldozer."

"So you see, Luigi, we only invited them for your sake," said Jimmy. "Besides, we ain't even sure if they're coming or not."

"Now let's go over the food again," said Blade.

"Yeah, I know," said Luigi. "You want Bellissimo sausages."

"But they have to share out absolutely equally," said Blade. "Between the twelve of us."

"Yeah," agreed Jimmy. "If anyone thinks they are getting a short portion, they can get quite emotional about it."

"But Boss," said Benni. "You don't know if there's going to be twelve people, or sixteen! Suppose the Gabrianni's turn up?"

"Yeah, they have to have a fair share too!" said Blade. "So whatever number of sausages you cook, it has to split fairly by twelve or sixteen."

"Oh boy!" muttered Luigi.

"I thought you said we could have sweet corn too," said Porky.

"Oh, yeah, we need lots of corn cobs, and they have to divide up fairly too!"

"Between twelve or sixteen?" asked Benni.

"No!" said Jimmy. "I just remembered something. If Half-smile Gabrianni comes, he can't eat sweet corn. On account of his half-smile, you see."

"Same as One Finger Jimmy can't play the violin," explained Benni exactly two milliseconds before his head collided with the wall. Jimmy's finger was right up his nose, which at least had the advantage of reducing the amount of Jimmy's breath Benni had to inhale.

"Why can't I play the violin?" asked Jimmy, with his eyebrows almost touching Benni's. "You wanna tell me, or do I push your eyes out from the inside?"

"Because, because..." whimpered Benni, "because nobody ever told you which end to blow down."

After a second, Jimmy relaxed.

"That's true," said Jimmy, wiping his finger on

Benni's hair. "If only I'd done music lessons instead of concentrating on delinquency."

"I know the feeling," said Blade. "Although I still get a kick from extortion, I sometimes figure that I'd have been happier as a professor of ancient Byzantine pottery."

Luigi wasn't listening, he had other things on his mind:

● How many sausages does he need to cook, so they can divide by twelve or by sixteen?

● How many corn cobs does he need, so they can divide by twelve or fifteen?

Let's deal with the sausages first, and there is a very simple answer! Suppose you multiply twelve by sixteen, then you know that the answer must divide by twelve or by sixteen! Let's check:

$12 \times 16 = 192$.

This works out because if only twelve guests turn up, they each get sixteen sausages. However if sixteen guests turn up, they each get twelve sausages. There's just one small problem...

YOU MEAN I HAVE TO COOK 192 SAUSAGES? CAN I COOK LESS THAN THAT?

To help Luigi out, let's find the smallest number that will divide by both twelve and sixteen. There is a name for the smallest number that other numbers can divide into and it is the *lowest common denominator*.

Because this sounds so horrid, it often gets shortened to the much zappier *LCD*. In this case we are looking for the LCD of 12 and 16, and once again we'll be using prime factors. At this point it's helpful to know that the prime factors of 12 are $2 \times 2 \times 3$ and the prime factors of 16 are $2 \times 2 \times 2 \times 2$.

What we do is "build" the LCD as we go along. We'll start by writing down the factors of our first number which is 12, so we put $2 \times 2 \times 3$. We then ask ourselves, "Does 16 have any factors that we haven't already written down?" We know the factors of 16 are $2 \times 2 \times 2 \times 2$, but we already have two "2"s written down. Because 16 has four "2"s altogether, we just tag two more on the end and get $2 \times 2 \times 3 \times 2 \times 2$. That's it!

To make it neater we can put the numbers in order so it reads $2 \times 2 \times 2 \times 2 \times 3$, and then before we multiply it out to get the answer, we can check it. First of all, we make sure our LCD has the factors needed to make 12 (yes, there they are: $\underline{2 \times 2} \times 2 \times \underline{2} \times \underline{3}$) and then we check it has the factors needed to make 16 (no worries: $\underline{2 \times 2 \times 2 \times 2} \times 3$).

Get ready for the exciting bit then, because when we multiply out $2 \times 2 \times 2 \times 2 \times 3$ we find that the LCD of 12 and 16 comes to 48.

These factors can tell you a bit more. How many times will 12 go into 48? All you do is cross out the factors of 12 in the LCD, so we cross out two of the 2's and the 3 like this: $2 \times 2 \times \cancel{2} \times \cancel{2} \times \cancel{3}$ We are left with 2×2 which makes 4. If you want to check, you will find that $12 \times 4 = 48$.

How many times will 16 go into 48? Again, cross the factors of 16 out of the LCD and you get $\cancel{2} \times \cancel{2} \times \cancel{2} \times \cancel{2} \times 3$ which just leaves 3. You'll find that $16 \times 3 = 48$. It's time to break the good news to Luigi...

- You only need to cook forty-eight sausages.
- If twelve people come they will each get four sausages.
- If sixteen people come then they each get three sausages.

"I'm going to cook forty-eight sausages," beamed Luigi. "It can't go wrong."

"Let's hope not, for your sake," leered Jimmy. "Believe me, I know what it's like to be wrong, because I was wrong once."

"Yeah?" asked Blade. "When?"

"It was a couple of years ago," said Jimmy. "Or maybe more, but it was a Wednesday, that's for sure. Well, Wednesday or Thursday, but I was down at Angels Dockyard, or was it the Mission House? Anyway, I thought I saw Bluetooth Fonetti eating a doughnut, but I was wrong."

"Hang on!" said Blade. "I remember that. It was definitely Bluetooth."

"Yeah," said Porky. "I remember it too. It had a jam centre with coconut flakes. It was definitely a doughnut."

"Oh! In that case I've never been wrong," said Jimmy.

"Apart from just then when you said you were wrong once," said Porky. "That was wrong."

"Hah!" said Jimmy. "In that case I *was* wrong once, so I was right after all, wasn't I, boss?"

But Blade's head was getting sore, so he decided to change the subject.

"So how many corn cobs you figuring on cooking, Luigi?" he asked in a rather tough-sounding voice to make himself feel better.

"I'm working on it!" said Luigi.

This time we're looking for the LCD of 12 and 15. Their prime factors are $2 \times 2 \times 3$ and 3×5 so let's build up an LCD again.

First we write down the factors of 12, so we put $2 \times 2 \times 3$. Then we know that the factors of 15 are 3 and 5, but as we already have a 3 written down we just tag on a 5 to get $2 \times 2 \times 3 \times 5$. Simple! All that's left to do is multiply $2 \times 2 \times 3 \times 5$ up and find that the LCD of 12 and 15 is 60.

We can check this LCD by making sure its factors include the numbers needed to make 12 (yes indeed: $\underline{2} \times \underline{2} \times \underline{3} \times 5$) and also check it has the numbers needed to make 15 (and yes again: $2 \times 2 \times \underline{3} \times \underline{5}$).

Luigi put down his pencil and looked up proudly.

"Sixty corn cobs!" he announced.

"Each?" asked Porky hopefully.

"No!" said Blade. "To share out!"

"Then can we have cannelloni rolls too?" asked Porky.

"Good idea!" said Jimmy. "Only don't forget that our cousin Lucretia sometimes won't touch them. It depends which dress she's trying to get into."

"That's true," said Blade. "So that means we'll need the right amount of cannelloni rolls to share between twelve of us, or eleven if Lucretia's being choosy, or sixteen if the Gabrianni's show up and Lucretia's not being choosy, or fifteen if they show up and she is being choosy."

"No problem!" said Luigi who was starting to get the hang of LCDs.

This time we are looking for the LCD of four numbers all at once, because we need a number that can be divided exactly by 11,12,15 and 16. We'll build our LCD up as before starting with the prime factors of 11. (This is rather jolly because 11 is actually a prime number anyway, so it only has one prime factor which is 11.) We write down 11.

Now we'll bring 12 in, and see what prime factors 12 has that we haven't already written down. Of course, the factors of 12 are $2 \times 2 \times 3$ and we've only written 11 down so far, so we have to put them all in. This gives us the LCD of 11 and 12 as

$11 \times 2 \times 2 \times 3$, but we can put the numbers in a more sensible order like this: $2 \times 2 \times 3 \times 11$.

Now we bring in 15 whose prime factors are 3×5. We already have the 3 written down, but we need to add in the 5. This gives us the LCD of 11,12 and 15 as $2 \times 2 \times 3 \times 5 \times 11$.

Finally we bring in the 16, whose factors are $2 \times 2 \times 2 \times 2$. We've already got two factor "2"s written down, but we still need to bring in two more. Finally, we get the LCD of 11,12,15 and 16 as $2 \times 2 \times 2 \times 2 \times 3 \times 5 \times 11$.

Luigi was starting to sweat as he multiplied the factors up.

"Oh me almighty!" he said wiping his forehead. "I make it two thousand, six hundred and forty cannelloni rolls."

"Each?" asked Porky again, but even he realized that he was starting to sound a tad greedy.

"Whatever," said Blade getting to his feet. "C'mon boys, time to go."

As the three men passed the counter, Jimmy turned back.

"Don't forget, Luigi," he snarled, "the food must divide up nice and equal otherwise this place becomes dust."

"So what you waiting for?" asked Porky. "Get on the phone and get it all ordered."

As the door closed behind them Luigi snatched up the phone.

"How we gonna cook up all those cannelloni rolls?" asked Benni.

"Quick!" said Luigi. "Get the shutters down, and pack the place up."

"Sure boss," said Benni. "But how's that gonna help?"

"I just thought of another number that divides equally between 11,12, 15 or 16."

"What's that?" asked Benni as he hurriedly wiped the counter.

"It's zero!" grinned Luigi. "If I order zero rolls, then they can all have the same, it don't matter who turns up. Same goes for the sausages, zero. And the corn cobs, a big fat zero. They can all have exactly zero of anything they like."

"So why are you on the phone, boss?" said Benni. "You don't need to make an order for zero stuff!"

"You're kidding!" said Luigi. "Of course I got to make an order! I'm ordering two airline tickets. By the time they get here tomorrow, you and me Benni, will be spending new year in Hawaii!"

THE PHANTOM SAUSAGE AND THE WRONG BOTTOM

When you're finding out about nice normal numbers you first sort out how to add and subtract, and then you go on to multiply and divide, and finally you go on to run a giant international bank and live in a mansion with helicopters and swimming-pools and you're allowed to stay up to watch telly as late as you want every night.

However, vulgar fractions are *not* nice normal numbers, and you'll have noticed that we've already sorted out multiplying and dividing them, but haven't really mentioned adding and subtracting yet. This is because adding and subtracting fractions is a bizarre and spooky thing to do, so before we hit it, let's get some willing volunteers.

When you two have quite finished, you're going to

help us check what we know about fractions so far...

To multiply fractions we just times the tops together and put the answer on top, then times the bottoms together and put the answer on the bottom.

$$\frac{4}{5} \times \frac{2}{3} = \frac{4 \times 2}{5 \times 3} = \frac{8}{15}$$

To divide fractions, you can just turn the dividing fraction upside down.

Oh yes we are, and then we can just multiply you together.

Shall we leave the sum looking like that? No, we can't resist it, so we'll polish it off.

$$\frac{4}{5} \times \frac{3}{2} = \frac{4 \times 3}{5 \times 2} = \frac{12}{10} = \frac{6}{5} = 1\frac{1}{5}$$

You'll notice we've started showing off a bit here. When we multiplied the tops and bottoms together the answer came to $\frac{12}{10}$, but we reduced it by dividing top and bottom by 2 to get $\frac{6}{5}$. Then we made it look more presentable by converting the improper $\frac{6}{5}$ to a nice mixed $1\frac{1}{5}$.

Yes, dealing with fractions is all fairly straightforward stuff, until you come across...

The phantom sausage

WAIT! Let's work it out with some maths first. What we are doing is adding $\frac{1}{2} + \frac{1}{2}$. Let's try adding the tops together and the bottoms together, and see what we get:

$$\frac{1+1}{2+2} = \frac{2}{4}$$

We get $\frac{2}{4}$. But just a minute! If you reduce $\frac{2}{4}$ by dividing top and bottom by 2, you get $\frac{1}{2}$!

So what has gone wrong here? It's time to use our secret weapon: *common sense*. If we add one half to another half, obviously we get two halves. In other words our sum should have looked like this...

$$\frac{1}{2} + \frac{1}{2} = \frac{1+1}{2} = \frac{2}{2} = 1$$

So when you are adding two fractions, just add the tops together, but keep the same bottom! Of course, that's simple enough – *providing the bottoms are the same to start with!*

Here are some sums using fractions with the same bottoms:

$$\frac{2}{9} + \frac{5}{9} = \frac{7}{9} \qquad \frac{10}{11} - \frac{4}{11} = \frac{6}{11}$$

How about $1 - \frac{3}{7}$? Although 1 isn't a fraction, you can easily make it into a fraction with any bottom you like. In this case it's handy to think of 1 as seven-sevenths, so we can write the sum like this: $\frac{7}{7} - \frac{3}{7}$ which comes to $\frac{4}{7}$.

As you can see, adding and subtracting fractions is easy – unless you've got...

The wrong bottom!

Let's have our two volunteers back and try to add them together.

Curses! But we mustn't let ourselves be beaten by two vulgar little fractions. What we have to do is give them matching bottoms and there's a simple way to do it. Remember that you can always multiply the top and bottom of a fraction by the same number. (This is usually called "multiplying through".) All we do is multiply each fraction through by the other fraction's bottom! We get:

$$\frac{4}{5} = \frac{4 \times 3}{5 \times 3} = \frac{12}{15} \quad \text{and} \quad \frac{2}{3} = \frac{2 \times 5}{3 \times 5} = \frac{10}{15}$$

You'll see that our two fractions each have the same value that they started with, because $\frac{12}{15}$ will reduce back down to $\frac{4}{5}$ if you wanted it to, and $\frac{10}{15}$ would reduce to $\frac{2}{3}$. However, because we've arranged for them to both have 15 on the bottom, we can add the new tops up. $10 + 12 = 22$. We just put this over

78

the 15 to get $\frac{22}{15}$ which becomes $1\frac{7}{15}$. Here's the whole thing written out:

$$\frac{4}{5}+\frac{2}{3}=\frac{12}{15}+\frac{10}{15}=\frac{22}{15}=1\frac{7}{15}$$

It might come as a shock that two simple looking fractions like $\frac{4}{5}$ and $\frac{2}{3}$ add together to make such an odd looking answer, but that's what murderous maths is like. Nobody told you it was going to be pretty.

How to get a smaller bottom

Sometimes when you add fractions, you end up with a massive big bottom which causes traffic congestion and can even be distinguished on photographs taken from outer space. Occasionally you're stuck with it, but usually you can make it a lot smaller.

Suppose we have $\frac{7}{9}+\frac{2}{15}$. We could multiply each fraction by the other's bottom and get $\frac{105}{135}+\frac{18}{135}$ but that looks far too murderous! Wouldn't it be great if there was a bottom smaller than 135 that we could convert both fractions to? Luckily there is one, and it's 45.

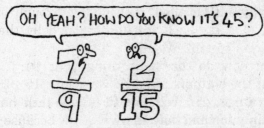

Because 45 is the smallest number that both your bottoms will divide into. DING! Where have we seen that before? Where did we find out about the smallest number that two other numbers will divide

79

into? It was in Luigi's diner! Yes indeed, the technical term for the smallest bottom is the *lowest common denominator* and 45 is the LCD of 9 and 15.

Now we know that the best new bottom is 45, we need to know what to put on the top. The main question is: what do we need to multiply the old bottom by to get the new bottom?

$$\frac{7}{9} = \frac{7 \times ?}{9 \times ?} = \frac{\text{new top}}{45}$$

So what do we need to multiply 9 by to get 45? If you know the times tables then the answer is obvious, but if not you just need to work out $45 \div 9$. Either way, it's easy to see that our mystery number is 5.

What we do then is multiply the top and bottom of our $\frac{7}{9}$ by 5 to get...

$$\frac{7 \times 5}{9 \times 5} = \frac{35}{45}$$

You now do the same thing with the $\frac{2}{15}$. Think about the bottoms: what do we need to multiply the 15 by to get 45? Well $45 \div 15$ is 3, so that's what we multiply top and bottom by.

$$\frac{2}{15} = \frac{2 \times 3}{15 \times 3} = \frac{6}{45}$$

To finish the sum, all we need to do is add up $\frac{35}{45} + \frac{6}{45}$ and get the answer $\frac{41}{45}$.

Smaller bottom short cuts

It all sounds a bit gloomy having to work out LCDs just so you can add up a few fractions, but with practice you'll often find you do it without even thinking. Look at this...

Suppose you have an ox that weighs $\frac{1}{8}$ of a tonne and a pig that weighs $\frac{1}{16}$ of a tonne. If you wanted to take them as hand luggage on an aeroplane, you'd need to know what they weigh together, so you need to work out $\frac{1}{8} + \frac{1}{16}$.

Remember that what you want to do is make both fractions have the same bottom and in this case there is a rather nifty short cut if you can see it! All you need to do is to multiply the $\frac{1}{8}$ through by 2. You get:

$$\frac{1 \times 2}{8 \times 2} = \frac{2}{16}$$

There! Now you can add your two-sixteenths to the other one-sixteenth and get the answer $\frac{3}{16}$. As it turns out, 16 just happens to be the LCD of 8 and 16, but when you're taking your ox and your pig on a plane with you, LCDs are unlikely to be your main concern.

Here's a slightly tougher example of a short cut: $\frac{3}{10} + \frac{4}{15}$.

In this case we can multiply the $\frac{3}{10}$ through by 3 to get $\frac{9}{30}$. We can then multiply the $\frac{4}{15}$ through by 2 to get $\frac{8}{30}$.

Hooray! We've converted both fractions to thirtieths, so we can add them together and get $\frac{17}{30}$. Once again it turns out that 30 is the LCD of 10 and 15, but we've already finished the sum without thinking about it. In case you're not sure about this, you could still do the sum the long way. Just multiply each fraction by the other's bottom and get a great big new bottom of 150 like this:

$$\frac{3 \times 15}{10 \times 15} = \frac{45}{150} \quad \text{and then} \quad \frac{4 \times 10}{15 \times 10} = \frac{40}{150}.$$

Add them up to get $\frac{85}{150}$, and then if you divide through by 5 you'll find it reduces to $\frac{17}{30}$.

You can always tell people who have spotted smaller-bottom short cuts because they spend all day walking round looking terribly pleased with themselves. Here's your chance to spot a smaller-bottom short cut as we take a break for a romantic interlude. Let's go and spy on the lovely Veronica Gumfloss in the pizza restaurant.

As you can see, even though she is terribly lovely, Veronica isn't exactly the brightest bulb on the Christmas tree. She didn't realize that if the pizza is cut into six, the pieces will be bigger than if it is cut into eight. However, in comes Pongo McWhiffy who also orders a pizza, which is cut into eight pieces. He catches the eye of the lovely Veronica and dazzles her with his roguish charm.

Of course Veronica cannot refuse such a dazzling offer, but here's an interesting question: who ends up eating more pizza?

- The lovely Veronica?
- Pongo?
- Or do they both eat exactly the same?

Before we work out the answer to the nearest cheesy crumb, this is one of those moments in maths when you can be a bit sneaky. If you think about it, $\frac{1}{6}$ of a pizza is bigger than $\frac{1}{8}$ of a pizza, isn't it? So if Veronica is daft enough to give away $\frac{1}{6}$ of a pizza and get $\frac{1}{8}$ of a pizza in return, she's going to lose on the deal and end up eating less, isn't she? There you are, you've already got the right answer without doing any sums! However, if you want to know exactly what's going on, then let's see how to do it...

What we want to know is how much pizza each person eats. Veronica's pizza was cut into six, but she gave a bit to Pongo, so she only eats five-sixths (or $\frac{5}{6}$) of her own pizza. However, she did get a bit of Pongo's pizza in return, but the trouble is that Pongo's pizza was cut into eight, so he gave her one-eighth (or $\frac{1}{8}$) of his. Although Veronica did get to eat six bits of pizza altogether, did she have...

- $\frac{6}{6}$ of a pizza, or...
- $\frac{6}{8}$ of a pizza?

Of course, as you've realized by now the answer is neither! You can't add one-eighth to five-sixths because it has got *the wrong bottom*. Here's the sum to work out: $\frac{1}{8} + \frac{5}{6}$. Now then, can you spot the short cut?

If we times 6 by 8 we get 48, so if we wanted we could work the sum out in 48ths. However, if you know your times tables you might realize we can use a smaller bottom because 6 and 8 both divide into 24, which happens to be their LCD. On we go then:

- To convert the $\frac{1}{8}$ into 24ths we have to multiply the 8 by 3 to make 24, so we multiply the 1 on top by this 3 too.

$$\frac{1 \times 3}{8 \times 3} = \frac{3}{24}$$

- When we convert the $\frac{5}{6}$ into 24ths, we have to multiply the 6 by 4 to make 24, so we multiply the 5 on the top by 4 as well.

$$\frac{5 \times 4}{6 \times 4} = \frac{20}{24}$$

- Finally add up the fractions:

$$\frac{3}{24} + \frac{20}{24} = \frac{23}{24}$$

This means that Veronica has eaten $\frac{23}{24}$ of a pizza, which is slightly less than a whole pizza.

We can now do the sum for Pongo. He eats seven

of his eight pieces, plus one of Veronica's six pieces, so Pongo gets $\frac{7}{8} + \frac{1}{6}$, which we can work out … but we don't have to bother!

There's another *easy* short cut! We know there were two whole pizzas to start with, and Veronica got $\frac{23}{24}$ of a pizza, so Pongo must have got what was left over.

Pongo got $2 - \frac{23}{24}$ pizzas!

To work this sum out we can convert one of the whole pizzas into twenty-fourths, so instead of 2 pizzas we have $1\frac{24}{24}$. It's now easy to take away the amount of pizza that Veronica got and see what Pongo got:

$$1\frac{24}{24} - \frac{23}{24} = 1\frac{1}{24}$$

This tells us that Pongo got a complete pizza plus a little bit extra.

And so just like many other beautiful relationships before and since, the love between Pongo McWhiffy and the lovely Veronica Gumfloss was doomed, all because of a few vulgar fractions.

Egyptian fractions

Ancient Egyptians had a special way of dealing with vulgar fractions, because they only ever allowed "unit fractions" which are fractions with a "1" on the top. Of course this was simple enough if they wanted to describe an amount such as $\frac{1}{4}$ or $\frac{1}{26}$, but what if they needed to describe $\frac{2}{7}$? They could have called it $\frac{1}{7}+\frac{1}{7}$, but they didn't allow themselves to use the same fraction twice, so instead they would call it $\frac{1}{4}+\frac{1}{28}$. If you want to work this out you get:

$$\frac{1\times 7}{4\times 7}+\frac{1}{28}=\frac{7}{28}+\frac{1}{28}=\frac{8}{28}$$

and if you divide through by 4 this gives you $\frac{2}{7}$. Phew!

This might seem like hard work, but the Egyptian way of working out sums was completely different to ours, and using unit fractions suited them better. Even today there are some very tough problems in maths and engineering which are made easier by using Egyptian fractions.

The only fraction that the Egyptians ever used that didn't have a "1" on top was $\frac{2}{3}$, which came in handy for bigger amounts. One example of this was found on an old scroll written thousands of years ago: it says that

86

if you divide seven loaves by ten men, each man gets $\frac{2}{3} + \frac{1}{30}$ of a loaf each. Does that seem fair to you?

By the way, as you might have guessed, mega brainy pure mathematicians absolutely love working out Egyptian fractions. Just for fun, if ever you meet some pure mathematicians, ask them how they are getting on with $\frac{3}{179}$. (This particular fraction has been melting their computers and giving them BIG headaches!)

The last blast

Oh no! You've just been taking your new cosmic phazmazycle for a spin round the galaxy, and what a great time you were having. You scorched past the Dog Star, screeched through the horsehead nebula and screamed round the Pleiades, but just as you were heading back to Earth you noticed the fuel gauge was flashing. You had got so carried away, you let yourself run out of petrol, so there was no choice but to make a crash-landing on the first solid world you met.

Stepping away from the sizzling zycle you look back at the seven-mile furrow you carved through the purple soil as you landed. At any other time you would be rather proud of it, but right now you are more concerned with finding the nearest garage. By an amazing stroke of luck, in the distance you see a small light flickering away. You make your way towards it, ignoring the rock mushrooms that gibber away as you pass. You approach a tumbledown shed and with a strange sense of foreboding you see the sign above the door: "Fiendish Fuels".

No! It can't be. Surely it must be another Fiendish – but of course it isn't. The door swings open and there in front of you stands your old arch enemy, Professor Fiendish himself.

"Har har!" he says, rubbing his hands gleefully. "Fancy you dropping in! And I know what you want."

"That's dashed clever of you." Your voice is loaded with high precision sarcasm and you intend to show no mercy. "Bearing in mind that the tank on my zycle is empty and I've walked to the nearest garage, what do you think it could be, oh great professor?"

"You need petrol," he replies smugly.

"You astonish me," you say. "So can I have some? And please, none of your weedy, diabolical tricks because I'm not in the mood."

"Oh dear!" sniggers the professor. "Who's feeling a bit touchy then? All right, I'll tell you what I'll do just for old times' sake. Look at this."

He opens a large door and inside are piled a selection of fuel cans.

"Help yourself," he says. "You can take any can you like, but just the one, no more."

"So what's the catch?" you say suspiciously.

"Well," says the professor, "since you ask so nicely, although the cans are all the same size, none of them are full. In fact, they all contain different amounts as indicated by the fractions written out on their sides. Your problem is that only the fullest can has enough petrol to get you home. If you pick the wrong can then you'll never make it and you will helplessly drift away into deep space."

So which can do you pick for the last blast home?

The best way to do this is to compare two cans at a time, and eliminate the one which holds less. Gradually you will eliminate all the cans except one, and so that will be the one with the most petrol.

The easiest pair of cans to compare first are the cans that hold $\frac{9}{13}$ and $\frac{10}{13}$, because obviously the can holding $\frac{10}{13}$ contains more. This means the can you want is definitely NOT the $\frac{9}{13}$ can, so we can eliminate it. Of course these two were easy to compare because the fractions were both "thirteenths" – in other words they both had 13 on the bottom. But how do we compare fractions with different bottoms?

We can compare some of these cans using common sense. Let's try $\frac{2}{3}$ and $\frac{3}{4}$ – which holds more? If you think about it, the $\frac{2}{3}$ can has one-third *missing*, and the $\frac{3}{4}$ can has one-quarter *missing*. One-quarter is smaller than one-third, so the the $\frac{3}{4}$ can has less missing – in other words it holds more! So we can eliminate the $\frac{2}{3}$ can.

The other way to compare cans is to make their fractions have the same bottom. If we compare the $\frac{3}{4}$ and the $\frac{2}{3}$ can this way, all we do is multiply each fraction by the other's bottom. The $\frac{3}{4}$ can becomes $\frac{9}{12}$ and the $\frac{2}{3}$ can becomes $\frac{8}{12}$. As we can see, the $\frac{3}{4}$ can holds $\frac{1}{12}$ more than the $\frac{2}{3}$ can.

So far then we've eliminated the $\frac{2}{3}$ can and the $\frac{9}{13}$ can. Let's look at two more cans. How about comparing the $\frac{7}{9}$ can and the $\frac{16}{21}$ can? We could mess about with LCD's if we like (the LCD of 9 and 21 is 63 if you're interested), but as we are not doing any fancy sums, we may as well just plough in and multiply each by the other's bottom. $\frac{7}{9}$ multiplied through by 21 becomes $\frac{147}{189}$ and $\frac{16}{21}$ multiplied through by 9 becomes $\frac{144}{189}$. Because 147 is bigger than 144, this shows us that the $\frac{7}{9}$ can holds more.

Let's compare some others

OH NO YOU DON'T. I'M NOT HAVING YOU GETTING THE ANSWER OUT OF SOME SILLY MATHS BOOK. YOU HAVE TO WORK IT OUT YOURSELF OR YOU WILL PERISH ALONE IN FREEZING SPACE! HAR! HAR! *Professor fiendish* x

And at last we have the final answer! The can that contains the most petrol is ~~NUMBER~~

Some good news

It's very unusual to have to play around with sums that mix up strange fractions such as $\frac{3}{11} + \frac{13}{14}$. Most of the time the fractions you'll come across are: $\frac{1}{2}, \frac{1}{3}, \frac{1}{4},$ $\frac{1}{5}, \frac{1}{6}, \frac{1}{8}, \frac{1}{10}, \frac{1}{12}, \frac{1}{20}, \frac{1}{50}$ or $\frac{1}{100}$, and it isn't very often they are mixed up in the same sum.

Some bad news

Very occasionally you will have to add up three different fractions at once, and you have to get an LCD for all of them. Here's an example: $\frac{2}{3} + \frac{1}{4} + \frac{4}{5}$

In this case you need the LCD of 3, 4 and 5. What do you think the smallest number that all three of these numbers can divide into is? Is it 12, 15, 20, 24, 30, 48 or 60?

If you work it out, you will see why adding more than two different fractions can be really murderous! Actually you would be very unlucky if this sort of sum ever turned up, and by a strange coincidence you would also be very unlucky if you ever found yourself having to work out...

The Fastbuck sewage disposal system

THE FASTBUCK GAZETTE
MUTANT FISH INVADE TOWN TOILETS

Yesterday it was reported that hideous yellow fish were leaping from lavatory bowls all over Fastbuck City. It seems that our beloved factories have been pouring so much toxic waste and radioactive sludge into the River Puke that the fish are mutating and starting to escape back up the city's sewer system.

"I had lifted the lid and was just turning round to sit down when I saw three purple eyes looking up at me!" said Mrs Offal of Gasmede Mansions.

"Next thing I knew, this fish had jumped out and was walking about on some hairy toes that were growing out of its bottom. It left a trail of slime along my bath mat and finished up burping up green maggots all over my towel rail."

A grim tale indeed, and it's all because the councillors of Fastbuck put profit before safety. Not surprisingly, the townspeople suggested that the authorities might like to consider some sort of emergency action...

...and so the councillors agreed to buy a purification system.

The day came for the grand opening.

94

What do you think? Will the machine be able to cope with both the toxic waste *and* the radioactive sludge at once? If not, how long will it be before the tank starts overflowing?

To work it out, the best thing is to see what happens in *one* day.

- The toxic waste can fill the tank in five days, so in one day it can fill $\frac{1}{5}$ of the tank.
- The radioactive sludge can fill the tank in seven days, so in one day it can fill $\frac{1}{7}$ of the tank.

● The machine can deal with a whole tankful in four days, so in one day it can get rid of $\frac{1}{4}$ of the tank.

This means that the amount of nasty stuff going into the tank in one day is $\frac{1}{5} + \frac{1}{7}$ tankfuls and the amount coming out is $\frac{1}{4}$ of a tankful.

Obviously if there's any left over, then the machine isn't able to work fast enough! The sum we need to work out is:

$$\frac{1}{5} + \frac{1}{7} - \frac{1}{4}$$

What we need now is the LCD of 5, 7 and 4 which turns out to be a rather impressive 140! The sum becomes...

$$\frac{28}{140} + \frac{20}{140} - \frac{35}{140} = \frac{28 + 20 - 35}{140} = \frac{13}{140}$$

Oh dear! At the end of a day, there will be $\frac{13}{140}$ of the tank that the machine has been unable to treat in time. Not surprisingly, the Fastbuck council have been too mean: their machine isn't big enough to cope!

So how many days will it be before untreated waste starts slopping over the sides of the tank?

Every day the tank fills up by another $\frac{13}{140}$, but how many $\frac{13}{140}$ are there in one tank?

To find the answer we need to divide one tank by $\frac{13}{140}$ so the sum is: $1 \div \frac{13}{140}$ which is the same as $1 \times \frac{140}{13}$ or just $\frac{140}{13}$.

If you work it out by dividing 13 into 140 you find that the tank will overflow in $10\frac{10}{13}$ days. There's nothing wrong in leaving the answer as $10\frac{10}{13}$ days, but it's more normal to work it out in hours and minutes.

What do you say?

Nonsense, it just needs a bit of common sense.

Oh, and of course it does tend to make us look rather brilliant.

First we'll write down the number of whole days in thick letters so we can easily find it again – **10 days** – and we'll work out what the remaining $\frac{10}{13}$ of a day is in hours and minutes.

There are 24 hours in a day, so $\frac{10}{13}$ of a day is $\frac{10}{13} \times 24$ hours which comes to $\frac{240}{13}$ or $18\frac{6}{13}$ hours. Now we'll write down the number of whole hours in thick letters – **18 hours** – and next we work out what the remaining $\frac{6}{13}$ of an hour is in minutes.

As there are 60 minutes in an hour we get $\frac{6}{13} \times 60$ which comes to $\frac{360}{13}$ or $27\frac{9}{13}$ minutes. Shall we work out the number of seconds too?

Good for you. Let's just make a note of the number of full minutes so we can find it – **27 minutes** – then, as there are 60 seconds in a minute, we just multiply that by the remaining $\frac{9}{13}$ of a minute to get $\frac{9}{13} \times 60$ which comes to $\frac{540}{13}$ or $41\frac{7}{13}$ seconds. Bah! You'll notice we're still left with a nasty little vulgar fraction.

Because $\frac{7}{13}$ of a second is so short compared to all the days, hours and minutes we've already calculated, we'll just ignore it! No – better still – as $41\frac{7}{13}$ is slightly closer to 42 than 41, we'll round the $\frac{7}{13}$ up to give us **42 seconds**. At last! Now we can look back at all the numbers we noted, put them together and tell the council that...

At least that gives the citizens of Fastbuck time to do something (such as run away as far as possible), and so once again another disaster is averted, all thanks to a bit of Murderous Maths.

DEADLY DECIMALS

There are one or two people who will be reading this book and thinking, "Why bother learning about all these sums when you can do everything on a calculator?" This is like saying "Why bother walking anywhere when you can ride on a bicycle?" or "Why bother wearing clothes when we've got skin?" Obviously it follows that if you are a calculator zombie, then you always ride a bike everywhere, and you never have any clothes on.

OF COURSE!

Although calculators are brilliant at bashing all sorts of big numbers about, their trouble is that they don't know when to stop. For those of us who have never been seen pedalling naked from the lounge to the kitchen, let's see how we would go about $17 \div 3$. We'll do it three ways: one with worms, one in our heads (which is the sensible way) and one using a calculator.

Worms first:

⅔ OF A WORM

Amazing how a chopped up worm can still wriggle, isn't it?

Now we'll try the second way of doing the sum in our heads, and it gives us a choice of two answers. Either we can have 5 with a remainder of 2, or if you like you can divide the last 2 by 3 which makes two thirds. This means the complete answer is $5\frac{2}{3}$.

Finally we'll do the sum with a calculator. Take all your clothes off (yes, and your pants too), get on a bike and start pushing those grubby little number buttons. Do you feel like a right ninny yet? If not you will do very soon. Put in $17 \div 3$ and what do you get? You get 5·666666666666666666 and if your calculator was a hundred miles long, the sixes would continue right to the end of the screen. The trouble is that the calculator hasn't the sense either to work out the remainder, or to give a nice neat fraction. All it can do is keep dividing for ever, which you have to admit is rather pathetic.

When calculators start to go mad…

To start with the calculator is quite sensible and does what we do – it tries to divide 3 into the "1" of 17. Obviously it can't go, so it moves along one place to find a "7" waiting there. It then tries to divide 3 into 17 and it gets an answer of 5 with a remainder of 2. That's exactly what we were doing when we did the division sum a few seconds ago, and being nice and sensible we knew what to do with the 2 left over – we either made a fraction or we just said we had a remainder of 2. Unfortunately the calculator is too stupid to think of that, so it just puts in a *decimal point* and keeps on dividing. If you want to know exactly what's going on, you'll find a full explanation in *The Essential Arithmetricks*, but right now the main thing to know is that the calculator is doing a sum that will never end. In the hands of a maniac, this could be *lethal*.

What should a decimal point look like?

In Britain the decimal point is written like this · or in other words it's like a full stop but floating up in the air a little bit. This rather cleverly avoids the decimal point being confused with anything else, but be careful! Other people mark it differently. For instance, Americans (and most calculators) write the decimal point down at the bottom like a full stop, and what's even worse is that in the rest of Europe they often mark the decimal point as a comma. As decimal points are so important, you'd think that everyone would use the clearest system, wouldn't you?

What does the decimal point mean?

As you probably know, if you have a "1" and want to multiply it by ten, you just move it one place to the left and put a "0" in the gap. What you've done is move the 1 from the units place to the tens place and that way "1" becomes "10". But what happens if you want to *divide* by ten? We'll need to get Wally the 1 to demonstrate for us.

When we divide Wally by ten, he has to move one place to the right. Off you go then, Wally.

That's the decimal point. As soon as you try to move to the right of the units place it suddenly turns up. Once you've crossed over the decimal point you'll become a fraction. Every place you move to the right makes you worth ten times less!

Wally's right, because he is now standing in the "tenths" place. By the way, you'll have noticed we've put a "0" in before the decimal point. We could have just put ·1 but because decimal points are so teeny it's sensible to put a 0 in front so that people realize there is a point there.

Thank you Wally for that top-quality contribution, but now we'll bring in some other numbers. If you have a number like 25·378, this is what it's worth:

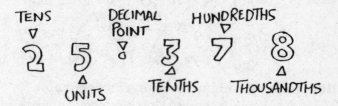

(Oh gosh! You should have been told before – you can get off your bike and get dressed again now. Sorry about that. Let's hope that not too many people happened to be peering in through the window. It's bad enough being naked on a bike, but if they knew that somebody called Wally the 1 had been explaining maths to you, you'd have to change your name and live under a bucket in a locked shed for years.)

By now you will have realized how crucial the decimal point is. If you send an order for 25·378 ice-creams, it means you want twenty-five whole ice-creams and a little bit more.

But what happens if you forget to put the decimal point in?

How to write vulgar fractions as decimals
There are some fractions that are easy to write in decimals. If you have a fraction of $\frac{7}{10}$, all you need to do is put 0·7 because as Wally showed us, the first

place after the decimal point represents "tenths". Hundredths are just as easy to write in decimals as tenths because you just move your numbers two places to the right. $\frac{3}{100}$ is 0·03. Of course thousandths, tenths of thousandths and so on are all just as easy.

Unfortunately, most fractions you come across will not be tenths or hundredths or thousandths, but converting them only requires a simple trick. You just pretend you haven't got a brain and *divide your vulgar fraction as if you were a calculator.*

Right then, let's bring on some vulgar fractions...

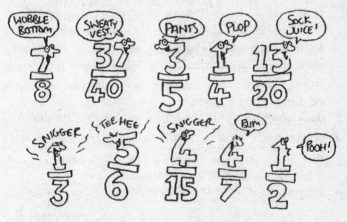

Behave, you lot, because we're going to clean you up. We'll start with $\frac{3}{5}$. All we do is treat it as $3 \div 5$ and work out:

$$\begin{array}{r} 0·6 \\ 5\overline{)3·0} \\ 3\ 0 \end{array}$$

Easy! The answer is that $\frac{3}{5}$ written as a decimal is 0·6.

- Here's how some slightly harder fractions come out:

$\frac{1}{4}$ is 0·25 $\frac{7}{8}$ is 0·875 $\frac{13}{20}$ is 0·65 $\frac{37}{40}$ is 0·925

Oo-er!

- Here's how some really miserable fractions come out:

$\frac{1}{3}$ is 0·333333 ... which you can write as $0·\bar{3}$ (The line over the top means that the last digit is repeated for ever.)

$\frac{5}{6}$ is $0·8\bar{3}$ $\frac{4}{15}$ is $0·2\bar{6}$

Eeek!

- Here's how an utterly depressing fraction comes out:

$\frac{4}{7}$ is 0·571428571428571 ... this one goes on for ever with the same pattern of numbers repeating, so you can write it out like this: $0·\overline{571428}$ and you put the line over the selection of digits that repeat.

Aaarrghhh!

- And here's how a *really simple* fraction comes out:

$\frac{1}{2}$ is 0·5

Phew!

Is your calculator cheapo or flash?

We don't like calculators much in this book, but because it's mainly their fault that we have to know about decimals, we may as well get them to help us out. The easiest way of converting a vulgar fraction to a decimal is to do the division on a calculator, and of course the calculator gives the answer as a decimal fraction. This can also be a good way of testing how clever your calculator is.

Put $2 \div 3$ into your calculator and see what you get:

Here we have two calculators showing slightly different answers, but which do you think is better?

CHEAPO kept calculating the sum and writing down sixes until it ran out of screen space, but then it stopped and threw away the teeny weeny remainder that was left. This was a bit naughty.

FLASH is better because it obeys the *"rounding off rule"* which is so important that it turns up in nearly all the other Murderous Maths books. What you're supposed to do is work out one more digit than you need to write down, and if that extra digit is a "5" or higher, you add one to the last digit. In this case FLASH realized that the extra digit would have been another "6" so it added one to the last digit and that's how the answer became 0·6666667. Doing this makes the answer a tiny bit more accurate.

How lazy are you?
With a lot of decimal fractions the numbers go on for ever, so calculators just keep going until they've filled up the screen. Of course, you're better than a calculator because you've got a brain and so you can choose how many digits you can be bothered to work out.

Suppose you have to work out $\frac{14}{17}$ as a decimal, what answer would you give?

- 0·8 Just one decimal place? It's amazing you can even be bothered to breathe.
- 0·82 Two decimal places means you probably don't bother getting undressed to get in the bath.
- 0·823 Three decimal places is better but it would have been even more impressive if you'd written down...
- 0·824 ...because you obeyed the rounding off rule. You went on to realize that the next digit would have been a 5 so you added one on to the 3 to make 4. If you did this, then well done, you're the sort of person who can survive without a remote control for the telly.
- 0·823529411765 Mathematically speaking, working to twelve decimal places is impressive. Your answer is accurate right down to the last millionth of a millionth – but at the same time maybe you should take a step back and try to look at your life in more general terms. Are you getting out enough? Are you meeting plenty of people, developing a range of interests, having a few laughs?

Just by way of interest, one of the greatest mathematical and scientific brains the world has ever known belonged to Isaac Newton who lived about 300 years ago. He liked working things out to over 50 places of decimals! Mind you he hardly had any friends, he didn't go out at all and all his wallpaper, curtains and cushions were bright scarlet, so there's a warning for you.

The good thing about decimals

As we found out in "The wrong bottom", when you add or subtract different vulgar fractions, you have to mess about to make all their bottoms the same. This can be a real pain if you have to add, for example, $\frac{9}{17} + \frac{21}{23} + \frac{3}{8}$. You end up with...

$$\frac{9 \times 23 \times 8}{17 \times 23 \times 8} + \frac{21 \times 17 \times 8}{17 \times 23 \times 8} + \frac{3 \times 17 \times 23}{17 \times 23 \times 8} = \frac{1656}{3128} + \frac{2856}{3128} + \frac{1173}{3128} = \frac{5685}{3128} = 1\frac{2557}{3128}$$

Even if you got that far, $1\frac{2557}{3128}$ is not exactly the cuddliest number to snuggle up to. You're better off putting your fractions into decimals first and getting: $\frac{9}{17} + \frac{21}{23} + \frac{3}{8} = 0.5294 + 0.9130 + 0.375$

(The first two of these decimals have been rounded off to four places, but the 0.375 worked out exactly, which was handy.)

You then just add up:

$$\begin{array}{r} 0.5294 \\ 0.9130 \\ + 0.375 \\ \hline = 1.8174 \end{array}$$

Money

There is one thing that we all know about that uses its own form of decimals and that is money. If you have £7.23, that means you have seven pounds and twenty-three-hundredths of a pound. However, as we know that there are 100 pennies in a pound, therefore one-hundredth of a pound is a penny. So if we have twenty-three-hundredths of a pound, we have twenty-three pence.

Suppose you have £3·78263726545. Obviously you've got three pounds, but how many pennies have you got? The answer is 78p, because money can only deal with two numbers after the decimal point. Sadly the other 0·00263726545 of a pound will be wasted and lost for ever.

BOO HOO!
BUT I WAS SAVING
UP TO BUY A BIKE.

Percentages

As you might already know, any number that is a "percentage" is actually divided by 100. It is very easy to imagine percentages as either vulgar fractions or decimals and you can choose whichever you prefer depending on what sort of mood you're in. Some days you might be in a vulgar mood, and others you might come over all decimalish.

If you are in a vulgar mood, you can convert percentages by just putting them over 100 – so for example 47% is the same as $\frac{47}{100}$.

However, if you are feeling decimalish, you just move the percentage two places to the right of the decimal point. In this case, if you have 47%, you can imagine it as 47·0% and when you convert it to a decimal you get 0·47. If you just have 3%, then it would become 0·03.

Percentages get used a great deal in shops, especially when they are having a sale. Because there are 100 pence in a pound, it makes it all quite easy to understand. For instance if something is 30% off, that works out that for every £1 you would normally pay, you save 30p. If you were buying a £5 pot of hairy green spot remover at 30% off, then you would save 5 × 30p which is £1.50 so you'll be left with enough to buy a big box of cornflakes. (Of course, you don't need to eat the cornflakes, but you can wear the box over your head until your spots have cleared up.)

The interesting thing about money

If you have loads of money then you can put it in an "interest" account at somewhere like a bank, and you will be given a bit of *extra* money every so often! The amount of extra money you get depends on the "interest rate". For instance, if the interest rate is 5·5% per year, then if you have £100 invested, after a year you will get £5.50 added on! For things like interest rates, you'll notice that percentages can also have fractions, in this case it's 5·5%, or if you're in a vulgar mood $5\frac{1}{2}$%. Obviously if you are lucky enough to be rich, you should look around and see who is offering the best interest rate before you invest it. You should also be careful, because sometimes people who offer you a better interest rate won't let you get your money back straight away when you want it, instead you have to wait for a

113

month or more. Like everything else in Murderous Maths, it pays to use your common sense.

One of the best things about percentages is that a lot of people use the words "per cent" to try to make themselves sound clever, but actually they end up talking gibberish.

What on earth is he talking about? If you convert two hundred per cent into a vulgar fraction, you get $\frac{200}{100}$ which comes to 2 so what he is really saying is:

Because percentages are a handy way of dealing

with all sorts of fractions, people tend to use them without thinking. This can lead to some odd mistakes.

Can you see what went wrong?

Answer: The first assistant correctly added 50% to £100 to make £150. However, when the boss asked the second assistant to knock 50% off, the second assistant did not know about the original price of £100. Instead he knocked 50% off the new price so £150 less 50% comes to £75. The boss should have made himself clearer!

The best offer

One last thought about money – if you know about fractions then you can work out the best offer in shops. Suppose you want some batteries and you know two shops who both sell them for £1 per packet, it doesn't matter which shop you go to. However, suppose one shop has a sign saying "Buy two packets, get one more free!" (This is the same as "3 for the price of 2".) Obviously this is good news – but then what if the other shop says "Buy one packet, get a second half price." Which is the better offer?

The thing to do is work how much you pay for *one* packet. In the first shop, you can get three packets for the price of two, which means that the price per packet is £2 ÷ 3 which comes to about 67p.

In the second shop you get 2 packets for the price of $1\frac{1}{2}$ packets. The normal price for $1\frac{1}{2}$ packets would be £1.50, so you're getting 2 packets for £1.50. This makes the packets cost 75p each. Therefore the other shop has the better deal!

(Of course, if you're only ever going to use two packets of batteries in the whole of the rest of your life, then you're better off spending £1.50 on two, rather than £2 on three and wasting the third!)

Decimal detectives!

Here's a calculator challenge for you. You start with some decimals and you have to work out which vulgar fractions they come from. Here's how it works…

Suppose you start with the decimal fraction 0·625. You need to find two numbers so that if you divide one by the other, that's the answer you get on your calculator. You might try 4 ÷ 9, but you will get 0·4444444 so that's no good. Maybe you'll try 5 ÷ 7 but then you'll get 0·7142857 so that's no good either. Eventually you'll find that when you put in 5 ÷ 8 you get 0·625, so the vulgar fraction you're looking for is $\frac{5}{8}$. You've cracked it!

Here's some more to try yourself, and to make it easy none of the numbers in the vulgar fractions are bigger than 9. You might like to use a pencil and paper to write down the numbers you've tried, and then the answer when you find it.

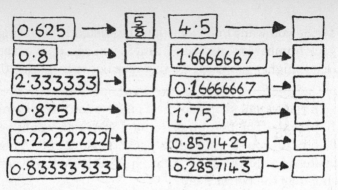

$0.625 \rightarrow \frac{5}{8}$ $4.5 \rightarrow \square$

$0.8 \rightarrow \square$ $1.6666667 \rightarrow \square$

$2.333333 \rightarrow \square$ $0.16666667 \rightarrow \square$

$0.875 \rightarrow \square$ $1.75 \rightarrow \square$

$0.2222222 \rightarrow \square$ $0.8571429 \rightarrow \square$

$0.83333333 \rightarrow \square$ $0.2857143 \rightarrow \square$

How are you getting on? You'll find that with only a little bit of practice, guessing which numbers you need gets very easy very quickly. By the way, if the answer fills your calculator screen, don't worry about the very last digit because it might be different depending on whether your calculator is Cheapo or Flash.

Once you've got good at this, you can battle it out with a friend! You'll each need a calculator, and you'll also need a bit of luck, a bit of guesswork, a bit of divine inspiration and a lot of skill to win!

- Each of you makes up a vulgar fraction using two numbers between 1 and 9. Write your fraction down, but don't let the other person see it! (For example you might write down $\frac{9}{8}$.)

- You each secretly make your vulgar fraction into a decimal on your calculator and write the answer down on a different bit of paper. (So you would put $9 \div 8$ into your calculator and write down the answer which is 1.125.)

- When you are both ready, you give your decimal number to the other person.

- The first person to work out the other person's vulgar fraction is the winner!

Soon you'll find this game is too easy, so you might

118

decide you want to make it harder. Instead of limiting your numbers to between 1 and 9, you can then agree to use higher numbers, for instance between 1 and 20.

ALL-OUT CALCULATOR WARFARE

If you tried playing "Decimal detectives" in the last chapter, you'll know that calculator challenges are immensely satisfying. At first you have several guesses that produce nothing like the answer you want – but then BINGO! When you do get the right answer and see all eight numbers slot exactly into place it's like winning the jackpot. Soon you'll be desperate to move into the big league where we play a much tougher game with serious rewards, and this is how it works.

What you need:
Two people can play, but it's better with three or more. Each person needs a calculator and a pile of solid gold coins. (If you can't be bothered to send your armed servants down to fetch the coins from your bullion vault, then you can use sweets or counters instead.) It's best if you all sit round a table with pencils and paper, and you have a plate or pot in the middle to act as the bank.

The object of the game:
You have to create your personal defence number by pushing any four buttons on your calculator followed by the = sign. (So you could push 5 ÷ 6 2 = and your defence number would be 0·0806452.) Other players will try and create this same number by pushing four buttons, and if they manage in time then you're *dead*.

What you do:

- To start with each player has to put *two* gold coins into the bank.

- Each player then secretly creates a defence number and must write it clearly on a piece of paper and place it face down in the middle of the table. (Each player should also make a private note of the four buttons that were pushed to create the number.)

- When everybody is ready, all the papers in the middle of the table are turned over to reveal the defence numbers.

- Players must attempt to crack the code for the other players' defence numbers! Choose whichever number you think looks easiest, and try to crack it first.

- If you think you can create one of the other defence numbers exactly, by pushing four buttons and the = on your calculator, you shout, "*Fire!*". Everybody else stops playing.

- You show which defence number you've cracked, and demonstrate which buttons you can push to create it.

If you are right, then that defence number is eliminated and you are awarded one gold coin from the bank. Everybody slaps their forehead and says "My goodness, you are brilliant" and

121

then everybody continues trying to crack the other numbers.

If you are wrong, then the defence number stays intact, and *you must pay* another gold coin into the bank. Everybody makes a rude noise in your direction and then play continues.

- All players keep playing until just one defence number remains intact. If your number is the last one to survive, then you win all the gold coins left in the bank, but...

- *Before claiming the coins, you MUST demonstrate which buttons you used to create your number!* If you cannot show how you made the exact number from pushing four buttons and the = sign, then the gold coins in the bank stay there for the next round. What's more, if you want to play in the next round it will cost you *five* gold coins instead of two!

Some vital details:

Just in case you end up having massive arguments in this game, here's some things to bear in mind:

- If your calculator screen is full, then only the first seven digits have to be exact – so if the number you were going for was 0·3529411 and you got 0·3529412 then you've cracked it!

- It doesn't matter if the four buttons you use are different from the four buttons the defender

122

used – so long as you get the right answer then you've cracked it. For instance $3\ 4 \times 9 =$ would give a number of 306, but you could also crack it with $5\ 1 \times 6 =$ or even by pushing $3\ 0\ 6\ \cdot\ =$

- People should only use the ten number buttons and the $+ - \times \div$ and decimal point buttons. However if everybody has a % button or a $\sqrt{}$ button then you can agree to use those as well.
- If there is more than one defence number left and nobody can crack them, then after an agreed time limit (say 5 minutes), the bank can be split between the survivors. However, they must each show how they created their defence numbers first!

Finally – a sneaky trick!

You can get the "square" of a number (in other words you can multiply the number by itself) by putting in the number, then $\times$ followed by $=$. For example if you put in $7\ 8\ 9 \times =$ you'll get a defence number of 622521. This will completely baffle anybody who does not know this short cut!

OF COURSE, AFTER A WHILE WE FOUND JUST PUSHING FOUR BUTTONS WAS TOO EASY!

SO WE PUSH FIVE BUTTONS TO MAKE OUR NUMBERS!

IT'S MURDEROUS FUN!

THE MEAN BITS

Welcome to Planet Mean. It's a rather spooky place because it looks exactly like Earth, and all the Meanies who populate it are exactly the same as the average human being. This all seems innocent enough but before you look round, prepare yourself for some gruesome shocks! There are one or two details that you should be warned about:

● Every Meanie has slightly less than ten fingers, and also slightly less than ten toes.

This strange fact is compensated for because...

● All Meanies have slightly less than two legs and two arms.

By now you will be starting to think that Meanies will look a bit incomplete, and you would be right. However, some younger Meanies look even more incomplete because...

● Each Meanie family has 2·4 children.

Can you imagine what having 0·4 of a child running around the house looks like? Yuk! Meanie parents don't look much better because of their bizarre dress sense:

● Every Meanie parent wears $1\frac{1}{4}$ trouser legs, a bit of a dress, high-heeled lace-up wellington boots, one sock and half a bra. In fact Meanie children can't tell their mum from their dad so they just mix their names up and either call them Dum or Mad.

Of course, if you really want to see some strange stuff, then visit a Meanie farm where all the animals look exactly identical. They are about the size of a goat, and all have about $3\frac{1}{2}$ legs and part of a wing. They are covered in a mixture of wool, fur and feathers, they lay bits of eggs and they all have a little udder with one teat on it.

Of course this odd view of life on Planet Mean could go on for pages, but we'll just look at one more strange fact.

● Every single Meanie dies at an exact age of 58 years, 4 months, 11 days, 5 hours, 47 minutes and 23 seconds.

So what is going on?

As we already know, a Meanie is *exactly* the same as an average human being. You'll see why the "exactly" part is important later on, but first we'd better get our heads around "*average*".

Poor old average

You've probably come across the word "average" before, but unfortunately it's often used to mean "boring" like this:

125

In other words the film isn't good enough to rave about, and it isn't even bad enough to have a good moan about. It's just average, and in a few weeks the kid will probably have forgotten he's seen it.

What average is really supposed to mean is "the most likely" or "in the middle of the range" so it's a bit unfair that people so often use it when they mean "boring". Quite often average things are the best, for instance an average banana split is not too ice creamy and not too bananary.

And when it comes to kissing, we can call on the lovely Veronica Gumfloss to demonstrate:

Averages can apply to almost anything. When most of us try to do things like learning French or playing tennis, we're not exactly brilliant but we're not too bad either so that makes us about "average". (Of course you might get the odd person who is amazing at maths but turns out to be useless at drawing, or you might have someone who's a wizard on the banjo but who couldn't make a sponge cake to save his life. For people who are really good at some things but pathetic at others, you might say it "averages out".) Other ways that averages turn up are the average number of segments you get in an orange, or the average time you have to wait for a bus.

If you know the "averages" of things, then you have an idea of what to expect out of life. Suppose your long-lost Auntie Thelma has just come back from discovering treasure in Dampest Nbonghe, as she walks in the door you're sure to be wondering how tall she is.

Before you see Auntie Thelma, you might well expect her to be about 1.65m tall, because that's the average height for aunties. Of course if she turns out to be 2.5m tall, you're in luck because you can dazzle her with a compliment like this...

There again if she was 1m tall you've still got a chance to make a pleasant remark...

Unfortunately it's more than likely that she'll turn out to be about 1.65m tall, but there's no harm in trying...

Nearly every feature of your own gorgeous self will be about average such as your weight, your braininess, the number of spots you've got, how many Christmas cards you received last year and so on. This might sound depressing, but that's the whole point of averages, they describe what most people and things are like. The fun bit is that everyone has *something* about them that isn't average, and that's what makes people interesting. Can you think of anything about yourself that is exceptional, wild, abnormal or bizarre – in other words it isn't average? Here are some thoughts...

● Can you run at 79 m.p.h.?
● Can you can eat six packets of crisps without a drink?
● Have you got three eyes?
● Can you talk six languages?
● Do you collect old toenail clippings?
● Are you 238 years old?
● Can you lick your tummy button?
● Is your favourite subject geography?

Apart from your exceptional features, everything else about you will be *about* average which is where the Meanies go wrong – because everything about them is *exactly* average.

Exactly average?

Hah! That made you sit up, didn't it? You thought that "average" was some sort of soft comfortable middle-ish thing that vaguely floated about smelling of warm bread, didn't you? Well you're wrong! This is Murderous Maths and we've got no time for waffle so we're going to grab this wishy-washy "average" thing, drag it to the laboratory, tie it to the bench, attach the electrodes and slice it right open from top to bottom. Yahoo! Look away if you're squeamish...

After close examination we find that there are three sorts of average called the *mean*, the *mode* and the *median*. We'll shove modes and medians into a specimen jar and analyse them later, because when people talk about averages, on average they'll be meaning the mean sort of average, so first of all we're going to see what the mean means.

The meaning of mean

The mean is an average number that is worked out exactly using a bit of adding up and division. The sums aren't too murderous, but like all maths, it's helpful to know why we are bothering to do them at all. There's no point wasting time in working out "means" if they turn out to be utterly useless, so let's have a ponder on what use "mean" averages are – and if we're going to ponder, let's ponder properly.

Ladies and Gentlemen – at this point in the proceedings Murderous Maths Incorporated is pleased to present for your delectation the official, government approved, scientifically accepted, ecologically friendly, politically correct...

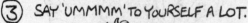

GUIDE TO PONDERING

1. HOLD YOUR CHIN WITH ONE HAND, AND SCRATCH YOUR HEAD WITH THE OTHER.

2. WANDER AIMLESSLY AROUND AN OVERGROWN MEADOW.

3. SAY 'UMMMM' TO YOURSELF A LOT.

UMMMM

Ooops! Watch where you're going...

THUD-DUNK

Oh dear, you've just dropped into a dank underground pit, and it seems that you are not quite alone...

You feel an itch running up to your armpit. You reach to scratch it and come away with a 52-legged purple and yellow goggbug sucking your finger. Just as you prise it off you feel something else burrowing into your sock! It's an orange toe-nosher with 46 legs – urgh! – but this is no time to be squeamish because a 34-legged druffpillar is nestling in your hair and crawling up your nose is a lime green bogiepede with 68 legs. A frantic tussle follows in which you remove them all, only to discover a 34-legged bellymite laying eggs in your tummy button.

You remove the bellymite with a quick flick of your tongue (it turns out that you are indeed exceptional, wild, abnormal and bizarre) and at last the five creatures lie twitching on the ground in front of you.

What a lovely collection! Of course, if you hadn't anything better to do, you might be wondering if they are poisonous, and if so did they bite you? Luckily for you, though, you do have something better to do because you were in the middle of a good ponder. A far more important consideration than mere life or death is: "What is the mean number of legs of these creepy-crawlies?"

You can work this out by counting up all the legs together, then dividing by the number of creatures. If you like you can write it out as a fraction like this:

Mean number of legs = $\dfrac{\text{Total number of legs}}{\text{Total number of creatures}}$

So add up the legs first: $52 + 46 + 34 + 68 + 34 = 234$ legs.

We now divide the 234 by the number of creatures, which is 5.

$234 \div 5 = 46 \cdot 8$ legs

OK, now you know that the mean number of legs per creepy-crawly is 46·8, but what use is that likely to be?

"Har har" comes a voice from above you.

You look up and, would you believe it, there's Professor Fiendish holding a large glass jar directly above your head. Doubtless it was he that dug the hole in the first place because that's just the sort of pathetic thing that would amuse him.

"Come to help me climb out, have you?" you ask sarcastically.

"Might do," replies the professor. "There again, I might not!"

"No surprises there then," you say with a sigh.

"Oh don't be like that!" says the professor. "Look what I've been collecting for you."

You realize that inside the glass jar, something is squirming about. In fact it isn't just something, it's a lot of things and they're not pretty.

"So you've got a jar full of creepy-crawlies?" you say. "Invited the family round, did you?"

"You won't think it's so funny when I tip all twenty of them over your head!"

Gulp! That's true, you won't think it's funny at all. But you know what the professor is like, he can't resist a challenge, so if you keep cool and calm then maybe you can talk yourself out of this mess.

"I tell you what," you say. "Let's make it interesting.

If I can tell you roughly how many legs are in that jar, you help me out."

"How many legs!" gasps the professor. "Legs? But how can you possibly know that?"

"Never you mind," you say. "Just get counting and see if I'm right!"

Above you the professor peers into the jar, and you hear him mutter:

"One, two, three ... stop squirming you fools! One, two, three ... I said STOP SQUIRMING..."

Luckily you've got a short cut, because you know the mean number of legs per creepy-crawly is 46·8. Of course there is no real creepy-crawly in the world that actually has 46 whole legs and also an extra 0·8 of a leg (unless it had had a nasty accident), but that doesn't matter. As long as you know the mean number, you can work out roughly how many legs there are in the jar. The professor accidentally told you the other thing you needed to know which is the number of creepy-crawlies he's got, so to get a reasonable idea of the total number of legs, you just multiply the mean number of legs per creepy-crawly by the total number of creepy-crawlies. You get $46·8 \times 20$ and it comes to 936. You shout upwards:

"How many legs do you make it?"

"I dunno!" he snaps back. "Hundreds I expect."

"Try 936," you say. "Give or take a leg or two."

"That can't be right," says the professor.

134

"Oh no?" you say. "Then take them out and count them properly!"

"Bah!" he mutters, and you hear him unscrewing the lid on the jar. Sometime later he is still counting.

"Four hundred and sixty-three, four hundred and sixty-four..."

"Cheer up!" you shout. "You'll be about half-way through by now!"

"That's what you think!" says the professor. "If you must know, this was the last creepy-crawly in the pot."

"Then the rest must have escaped!" you say.

"Escaped?" gasps the professor. "Where to?"

But his scream suddenly answers his own question.

"Argh! Get them off me! They're creeping in my ears and crawling under my vest."

"So you've found them then?" you remark, but he doesn't hear you.

By now you've managed to scramble to the top of the hole, just in time to see him run off and dive headlong into a river. Another fiendish challenge defeated!

So did you get the answer right?

You stand on the riverbank and look down as the professor slowly drifts away to sea. You can't tell whether he is waving at you for help or frantically scratching himself to shreds, but this is no time to consider such trifles. A far bigger question is niggling you – how close was your answer of 936 legs?

Your original calculation of the mean was based on five creepy-crawlies, which had 52, 46, 34, 68 and 34 legs. If the professor's jar contained a similar assortment of creatures, then your answer would have been quite close. However, if all twenty of the creepy-crawlies in the professor's jar had been bogiepedes with 68 legs each, there would have been 20 × 68 legs in the jar – this comes to 1,360 legs which is quite a lot more than your answer. On the other hand, if the professor had collected twenty bellymites with just 34 legs each, there would only have been 680 legs in the jar which would have been a lot less than your answer. Of course you had no way of knowing what was in the jar, so you gave an answer that was somewhere in between the two – and of course that's what working with averages is all about.

Generous or mean?

Sometimes when you have a group of numbers, it's handy to know the mean so you can tell which numbers in the group are higher or lower – which is what happened on Veronica's birthday. All her doting admirers put some money towards buying her a present (because she is so terribly lovely) and here's a list of how much each person contributed.

SIDNEY OLDSOCKS	52p
BERTIE BIKECLIPS	75p
PONGO McWHIFFY	7p
RODNEY TUFT	46p
WAYNE W. WAYNESON	82p
MALCOLM PITSTAIN	69p

Veronica worked out the "mean" contribution by adding up all the money, and dividing by the number of people. She found it came to £3.31 ÷ 6 which makes 55·17p per person. (In this chapter we'll round everything off to two decimal places if that's OK with you.)

This is crucial information to Veronica because now she knows who gave *more* than the mean...

And who gave less...

137

And as for one person...

Teachers are very fond of working out the mean of class results (although a lot of them won't admit it). That way they can tell who is doing better than average and who is not. By the way, if ever you catch a teacher moaning like this:

HALF OF MY CLASS ARE BELOW AVERAGE.

You can reply...

OF COURSE THEY ARE! OTHERWISE THE AVERAGE WOULDN'T BE THE AVERAGE WOULD IT?

A thought about sport
Sporty people in particular are very keen on the mean type of average because they use it to see if they are getting better. It works like this:

Back to the Meanies

If you are still wondering why the Meanies are like they are, then here's a question to get you started:

What is the mean number of fingers each person in the world has?

Do you think the answer is ten?

No, it isn't. The sad fact is that the mean number of fingers per person is *not* ten because although most people do have ten fingers, there are a few people who have some fingers missing. If you counted up all the fingers in the world and then divided by the total number of people you would get an answer that was slightly *less* than ten!

WEE-YAW-WEE-YAW!

Gosh, what a racket! Just when things are getting interesting too. In case you're wondering what's going on, a police van has just pulled up. Hey officer, do you mind keeping the noise down? We're trying to read a book here.

Oh well, since they're here, we may as well use them. It turns out there are six men in the back of the van known to the authorities as Numbers, The Weasel, Chainsaw Charlie, Blade, Half-smile Gabrianni and Porky. If they all hold their hands out, we can see they have ten fingers each, which makes sixty fingers in total. To get the mean number of fingers on each person, you divide this total by the number of people which is 6. Surprise surprise, you find $60 \div 6$ comes to 10, so the mean number of fingers on each man is ten.

Hello! Here comes another cop with the last member of the bunch.

This makes life interesting for us! Hold your hands out guys – because if we count up the fingers again, we get 61. (Jimmy only has one finger since he lost the others in an unexpectedly vicious game of snakes and ladders.) We now have seven people to divide by, so the mean number of fingers of all seven is $61 \div 7$ which makes 8·71. You'll see that when we include One Finger Jimmy, the mean value has come down.

It's the same with the whole population of the world. Even if only one person had just one finger missing, the mean number of fingers that everybody would have is reduced from exactly 10 down to about 9·9999999998 – in other words *less* than ten! And so it is that Meanies all chop a little bit of finger off, because they like to be *exactly* like the *average* human being.

Meanies do similar sums for everything else. Even when it comes to something silly such as how many socks they should wear, they count up how many socks are being worn all over the world and divide that by the total number of people and that's how come they only wear one sock each. Anyway, that's enough about means and Meanies for now, so let's check out those other two things that we stuffed into specimen jars.

Are you in the "mode"?
Some years ago, people used to say "the mode" when they were talking about fashion. If you dressed yourself up in purple velvet flares, massive platform shoes, a very woolly coat and a big floppy hat with a flower sticking out of it, people would say "Gosh, aren't you trendy?" or "My oh my, you're all the rage," or even "Ooh! You're really in the *mode*." (It goes without saying that you'd also have to be in a

143

pretty strange *mood* to wear that lot, but that's fashion for you.)

Mathematically speaking, the "mode" is the most common item to appear in a group and in the 1960s so many people dressed themselves up like this, that it became "the mode". Yes, nearly everybody was doing it, but if you find it hard to believe then go and dig out some old family wedding pictures – you'd be amazed at what some of your fuddy old relatives used to wear.

Remember the five creepy-crawlies you found in the underground pit? Although the *mean* number of legs was 46·8, the *mode* number of legs was 34, because more creepy-crawlies had 34 legs than any other number. In fact as creepy-crawly fashion goes, 34 legs is dead cool.

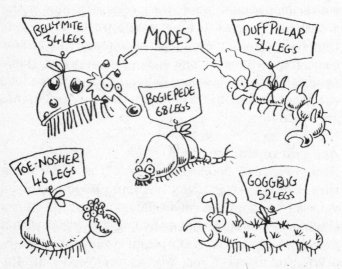

Even though the mode and the mean are both types of averages, they can give you very different results. Suppose we shove 3 one-legged bottigrubs in with our creepy collection:

- the mean number of legs of all eight beasts will be $52 + 46 + 34 + 68 + 34 + 1 + 1 + 1$ divided by 8 which comes to 29·63.
- the mode number of legs is 1, because that's the number that the most creatures have.

The great thing about modes is that hardly any maths is involved. With "means" you have to add up and divide but with modes the toughest thing you need to do is a bit of counting. There are also things you can do with modes that you cannot do with means.

Suppose you look through the rubbish bag at the back of the charity shop and find five blue socks, three yellow socks and seven green socks...

I DON'T THINK WE'LL BE NEEDING THESE...

- What is the mode colour of sock? The answer is green, because that's the colour you found most of.
- What is the mean colour of sock? Of course that's a ridiculous question, because you can't calculate the mean of a set of colours.

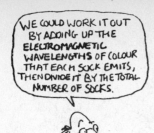

When you're using averages, the mode can do a slightly different job from the mean. Suppose you found one extra sock, what colour is is likely to be? The answer is green, because green is the mode – in other words green is the most common colour for socks that are stuffed in rubbish bags at the back of charity shops.

If Meanies had any sense, they would stop being Meanies and start being Modies because then they could have ten fingers and also two arms and two legs! That's because the majority of people have a complete set of everything which makes it the mode. Mind you, if the Meanies did decide to become Modies, they would all be female, because slightly more of the population are female than male. (Meanies would probably be very glad to be female, because at the moment they are a mean mixture of both female and male! In fact if you think about it, Meanies must find *bathroom activities* a bit confusing.)

Meet the median

Finally, we meet the third sort of average. The median is "the one in the middle". Let's invite our five creepy-crawlies back on to the page for a last look...

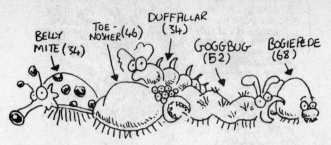

BELLY MITE (34)
TOE-NOSHER (46)
DUFFALLAR (34)
GOGGBUG (52)
BOGIEPEDE (68)

The median creepy-crawly is the toe-nosher. This is because two of the creepy-crawlies have more legs, and two of the creepy-crawlies have less, so he is the one in the middle. Again, you don't need to do any fancy maths to work this out, just a bit of simple counting!

You will usually find that the median value is close to the mean value. If you check our little friends here, the median value (i.e. the number of legs on the toe-nosher) is 46, and we saw the mean value is 46·8 so those two results aren't very far out. If you haven't time to do tons of adding up and dividing to get a proper mean value, quite often you can do a sneaky short cut by finding the median value instead.

Right, we've finished with the creepy-crawlies, so let's slam the book before they creepily crawl out and attack us.

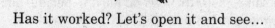

PAP!

Has it worked? Let's open it and see...

That's better!

Now let's look at Veronica's birthday contributions again. (We'll put them in order of generosity to make it easier):

Wayne W. Wayneson	82p
Bertie Bikeclips	75p
Malcolm Pitstain	69p
Sidney Oldsocks	52p
Rodney Tuft	46p
Pongo McWhiffy	7p

Who do you think gave the median amount of money?

We are looking for the person who's contribution comes in the middle but we've hit a small problem. If you're finding the median of an *odd* number of things then it's very easy – for instance when we found the median of the five creepy-crawlies earlier, it was obvious which was the middle one. Unfortunately, here we have an *even* number of things to deal with, so who do you think is in the middle – Malcolm or Sidney? In some cases this can be hard to decide, but luckily here we have a *freak*.

A freak is a number in a group that is either far bigger or far smaller than the others, and so it can have a misleading effect. A few pages ago we worked out that the *mean* contribution each boy made was 55·17p. However, this is a bit unfair because if it hadn't been for Pongo's miserable little 7p, the mean contribution would have been quite a bit higher. Let's suppose Pongo wasn't involved and see what the mean for the other five would have been. The sum is $(82 + 75 + 69 + 52 + 46) \div 5$ which comes to 64·8p. Gosh, when you don't count Pongo it looks like the other five have all given nearly 10p more! Because freak numbers give misleading answers, it's often helpful to ignore them.

Yahoo! Now we know about ignoring freaks, let's ignore Pongo which just leaves us with the five other desperate Veronica fans and it's obvious that Malcolm is the one in the middle, so the median value is 69p.

Once you've found a median, you can use it in the same way as a mean. Suppose Veronica had 30 boyfriends all contributing to her birthday fund, how much money could she expect? The median contribution was Malcolm's at 69p, so just multiply

69×30 to get an answer of £20.70.

Remember the mean value (which included Pongo's feeble contribution) was 55·17p, so if we had used that to work out how much Veronica might expect from 30 boyfriends, we would have got $30 \times 55·17p$ which is £16.55.

Don't blame the maths – blame Pongo!

How to check a till receipt quickly
How many times have you seen this happen?

150

Well, with this trick you'll be able to say:

Of course it takes ages to add up loads of numbers, especially in your head, but luckily averages can give us a quick rough way of checking. All you need to do are two simple things:

First... Ignore all the pence, just add up all the pounds. This is quite easy because not many things cost more than £2, so you can quickly work down the list and do it in your head. (Don't add on anything for items costing less than a pound.)

Then... Fold the receipt in half, then count up how many items there are on one half of the receipt. Add this number to the number of pounds.

The answer will be the approximate total in pounds of everything on the receipt!

So how does this work? The first step of adding up all the pounds is obvious, but once you've done that you need to get a rough idea of what the total number of pence in all the prices comes to as well. (Therefore if something on the list was £2.38, as you've already counted the £2 now you just need to put the 38p into your calculations.)

Here's the clever bit: the average number of pence in each price is about 50p. Of course some prices will have a high number of pence such as 98p, and others will have a low number like 15p, but roughly speaking they will average out at 50p. This means that after you have counted up the pounds, you then add on 50p for every item on the list. The short cut here is that instead of counting up all the items and adding 50p each, you just count up half the items and add £1 each.

There you are!

There's just one thing to be aware of, and that is your answer will usually be a little bit low because the average number of pence in prices is more like 60p than 50p. This is because supermarkets like charging prices such as £2.99 rather than £3.00 because although it's only 1p less, they think it looks a *lot* cheaper. Consequently you end up with more high numbers of pence than low numbers, and that makes the average number of pence in prices a bit higher than 50p. Don't worry about it though, as long as you tell people that you're just working the total out roughly, you'll still be able to impress them. Besides, if you want to be flash you can always add an extra pound or two on the end to compensate for the difference!

How to count all the words in this book

Here's another way of using averages that the people in the Murderous Maths factory use all the time. All you need to do is count the words on one page, then multiply by the number of pages.

WHICH PAGE DO I COUNT THE WORDS ON?

Good question. You'll see some pages in this book are nearly all full of writing, and other pages have lots of pictures. What you need to do is find a page such as this one which has an "average" mixture of both. If you flick through the book, you'll find that about $\frac{2}{3}$ of it is writing and $\frac{1}{3}$ of it is pictures, so this is a good one to count as it is about $\frac{2}{3}$ full of writing.

If you want to be technical, you might say that this page has an average number of words on it. You then count the words on the page.

IT'S A LOT OF WORDS TO COUNT!

Yes, of course it is, so what you might like to do is count the words on ten lines, then divide by ten. That way you'll get a *mean number of words per line*. You then count how many lines are on the page, and multiply the number of lines by this mean number. You'll end up with a reasonably accurate number of words for the page! Just multiply this by the number of pages and you've got your answer.

Here's what to do again, step by step:

1 Find an average page.
2 Count up the words on 10 lines.
3 Divide the answer by 10 to get a mean number of words per line.
4 Count the lines on the page.
5 Multiply together: the mean number of words × lines on the page × number of pages.
6 The answer is roughly the total number of words in the book!

Of course this system works with any book, even great big long ones.

How clever are authors?

You can also use averages to find out how clever the author of a book is. This is because brainy authors tend to use really long words and come out with stuff like "...postulating established authenticity propounded by integrating conventional hypotheses alongside lateral ideology...", whereas simple authors just write things such as "d is for dog".

What you need to do is work out the *mean number of letters in each word*, which is dead easy:

Find a section that has 10 words in it. Count up the total of letters in the ten words, and divide by 10 – and that will give you the mean number you want. If you want to be more accurate, count up the letters in 20 words, then divide by 20, or better still count the letters in 100 words and divide by 100! The more words you count, the better your answer will be. You can then compare your answer to this table:

MEAN NUMBER OF LETTERS PER WORD.	NOISE YOU'D GET IF YOU TAPPED THEIR HEAD.	BRAININESS OF AUTHOR.
Under 3·0	PINGLE-ING	Probably writes with a wax crayon all over the wallpaper.
3·0–3·6	PANK	Only allowed to use scissors if a responsible adult is present.
3·6–4·3	PLONK	Able to watch daytime telly without screaming.
4·3–4·74	PLUPP	Not able to watch daytime telly without screaming.
4·75	PUK	Well informed, astute, charming, handsome, witty without being overbearing, pleasant and disarmingly modest.

155

4·76–5·3	PUDD	Doesn't just write books, also reads a few.
5·3–6·1	PUTT	Gets invited to make speeches at posh dinners.
6·1–6·8	PURP	Very difficult to stop this person making a speech at a posh dinner (or anywhere else for that matter).
6·8–8·0	PLAPTH	Can't order a pizza without a long angry queue forming behind this person.
8·0–20·0	POW! CENSORED	Warning – don't tap this person's head because it is so jammed full of brains it will probably burst open.
Over 20·0	PINGLE-ING	Probably no brain at all because this person doesn't realize that you have to put gaps between words.

If you want to know how brainy the author of THIS book is, this sentence conveniently contains exactly twenty words.

THE TERRIBLE TEST

By now you will have seen the answers to the terrible test on the very back page of this book. Gosh they look tough, don't they? But if you remember, back at the beginning of the book you were given a guarantee that you would be able to impress even the most obnoxious person by being able to work out all those answers in your head!

Now's the time to see if you can do it, so here come the questions. Good luck!

1 Which of these numbers does NOT fit into this sequence?

   1, 2, 3, 86·77561, 4, 5, 6

2 Calculate: $2{,}583{,}900 + 1$

3 The Shimura-Taniyama conjecture was a vital step in the solution to Fermat's last theorem. How do you spell "The Shimura-Taniyama conjecture"?

4 Two rockets flew to the planet Zog. The first took 3 years, 9 months, 1 week, 4 days, 11 hours, 52 minutes and 14 seconds to get there. If the second one took 10 seconds longer, how long did it take?

5 Which of these fractions takes the longest to write out?

   $\frac{4}{5}$ $\frac{1}{11}$ $\frac{355624}{1000927}$ $\frac{5}{6}$

6 If you check carefully, you'll see that the answer to this sum has a mistake in it. What should the answer really be?

   $15{\cdot}978 \div 2{\cdot}114 = 7{\cdot}55\text{mistake}818538$

7 Which of these numbers is the biggest?

   $3, 8, 26, 297878^{39{\cdot}66}$

GOODBYE... AND DON'T FORGET TO SHUT THE BOOK!

There! You've completed the *terrible* test! How did you get on? If you got all the questions right then well done. Don't forget to go round showing everybody the answers (although it's better to keep the questions secret) and you'll have great fun saying: "This is the sort of thing that I can work out in my head." They might not believe you, but that's their problem. You know you're telling the truth, so that's what matters.

As you can see, we've just about come to the end of this book and you must admit that we've every reason to be proud of ourselves. Together we've trawled through some of the very meanest and vulgarest bits to be found in Murderous Maths (or any other subject for that matter), and let's face it, some of it was not pretty! There are a lot of people who would run away screaming at the first sight of something like this...

SO YOU THINK YOU CAN CANCEL ME OUT, DO YOU?

SNIGGER

SNIGGER

...but Murderous Maths readers don't know the meaning of fear.

Not only have we learnt how to handle ourselves in the face of some tough opposition, we've also had a lot of fun, so thanks for coming along and making it into a party. Before you finally put this book away though, do make sure it's firmly closed. We don't want any nasty little items escaping!

Hopefully we'll all meet up again in another book, but until then here's a thought to keep you going:

What is the oldest, biggest, purest and most useful subject across the entire universe and indeed any other universes that may exist?

You guessed it – Murderous Maths!

Answers to the terrible test

1 86·77561

2 2,583,901

3 The Shimura-Taniyama conjecture

4 3 years, 9 months, 1 week, 4 days, 11 hours, 52 minutes and 24 seconds

5 $\frac{355624}{1000927}$

6 7·55818538

7 $297878^{39·66}$

How many did YOU get right?